THE BEGINNER'S GUIDE TO
HUNTING
+
FISHING
IN NEW ZEALAND

Hunting&Fishing
Hunting&Fishing

THE BEGINNER'S GUIDE TO HUNTING + FISHING IN NEW ZEALAND

PAUL ADAMSON

A RANDOM HOUSE BOOK published by Random House New Zealand
18 Poland Road, Glenfield, Auckland, New Zealand

For more information about our titles go to www.randomhouse.co.nz

A catalogue record for this book is available from the National Library of New Zealand

Random House New Zealand is part of the Random House Group
New York London Sydney Auckland Delhi Johannesburg

First published 2013

ISBN 978 1 77553 512 6

Design: Kate Barraclough
Front cover photographs: left and top left, Mike Heydon; top centre and right, Photos.com; bottom right, Paul Adamson; bottom centre, Photos.com
Back cover photographs: bottom left, Mike Heydon; remaining photographs, Photos.com
Front flap: Mike Heydon
Back flap: top, Mike Heydon; bottom, Photos.com

Printed in China by RR Donnelley Asia Printing Solution Limited

To our sons James and Tom,
who have grown into fine men
as they measured themselves
against all the outdoors has
to offer.

May the mountains, rivers
and seas always treat
you well.

INTRODUCTION

We are incredibly lucky to live in a country with so many opportunities to enjoy the outdoors. From alpine conditions in the South Island to low-lying bush-clad hills in the North Island, the New Zealand landscape can be as spectacular, challenging and dangerous as any in the world. We can visit any of our rivers, rushing through huge gorges or gently winding through farmland towards lake or sea, and benefit from their pristine waters. It is no wonder that New Zealand has one of the highest numbers of hunters in the world per capita. Whether from mountain, coastline, plain or bush, we can spend all of our lives enjoying the natural bounty available to us: hunting and fishing are terrific activities, and I hope that this book will help you discover what is out there and how you can become involved.

Safety is very important wherever you hunt or fish. A great rule to follow is: 'If you don't know, ask.' This book is a beginner's guide to hunting and fishing. I want you to have fun learning to hunt for rabbits, or for that giant eel in the farm drain, and enjoy the thrill of the hunt which drives us to check that next stretch of water or that next ridge, but I also want you to stay out of harm's way. It is vital to know how to go into our mountains, what to do when you are near water, and how to handle and use a gun safely. Many tragic deaths and accidents could be avoided if everyone made sure they followed firearm rules and guidelines.

There are many different approaches to hunting and fishing. This book cannot cover everything, nor provide details on how to go about catching every species, but we will cover 11 key areas that can be enjoyed by those of any ability. Key words are in **bold red**, and are defined at the end of each section. If killing isn't for you, there are other options. Perhaps target shooting could be right up your alley and blossom into a serious sporting activity, or take a photograph of the fish you have caught before releasing it back into the wild. If you prefer to hunt with a camera, the book will provide you with ideas to explore animals and their habitats. Some readers may be interested in only one particular area, such as hunting difficult-to-catch whitebait (watch out, this can easily become an obsession for some). Whatever your interest, you can dip into a specific chapter or read the book from start to finish. I want to provide enough information to help you, the hunter, enjoy the activity safely and experience the great anticipation of hunting and fishing.

Being a responsible hunter and behaving ethically is also very important. This means that no one should hunt with a firearm and shoot at animals unless they have practised on targets and can achieve clean, one-shot kills at different distances. A responsible hunter will use a well-trained dog to assist in spotting animals, and in the case of small game the dog will be able to find and retrieve animals if they are wounded. Every effort should be made to make use of the animal taken, especially when you have shot to eat. I have included some recipes I have often used, and encourage you to create your own dishes. Remember that family pets can also enjoy any fish or meat offcuts. Decorative skins for the floor or wall can be made, or duck, pheasant or stag heads can be prepared, stuffed and mounted.

Always buy a hunting licence, as the money you pay for it will go towards protecting and maintaining habitats and help increase fish and animal numbers. It is very important to remember future generations who will get to enjoy hunting and fishing only if we make sure our land and waters and all of their inhabitants are managed sensibly. Make sure you know how many animals you are allowed to take or how many fish you can catch.

Finally, remember that some days out hunting or fishing will never be repeated. When everything goes perfectly, when the wind is in your favour and the stalk is sublime, leading to a precise shot dropping the animal in its tracks, when the fish are in a fury to get on your hook, when the ducks are raining in to the decoys and your wing-shooting positively nails them 'dead on arrival', when the whitebait, a mass of silvery delicacies, fill the net— soak it all up, because these moments are pure gold.

There will be plenty of times when you come home empty-handed, and that is absolutely fine — after all it is the wonderful lure of the outdoors and the anticipation of the hunt that drives us to venture out again and again.

When are you heading out next?

BEFORE YOU READ THIS BOOK

These are some basics of safe gun handling that have to be followed **at all times**. Make sure you read and understand the *Arms Code — Firearms Safety Manual*, published by the New Zealand Police, before handling firearms.

Always have a gun-licensed adult with you if you are under 16 or do not hold a firearms licence.

Know your firearm well. Get to know your gun thoroughly before going out on a hunt — especially the location of the safety catch, its firmness and any issues around loading and unloading. Note also that the safety catch should be tested beforehand. Be aware of the gun's recoil and how different shooting positions can affect your control after firing.

Familiarise yourself with the trigger pressure before actually shooting at animals. A quick way to miss — or worse, wound — an animal, is to have a round exit the barrel before you have aimed properly. A shot getting away on the hunter rarely results in a clean, one-shot kill.

Know the distance at which your firearm is effective and your own skill level in putting shots right where you want them on the target. This takes lots of practice, but you need to understand how your firearm works before heading out on the hunt.

Unload the firearm by removing any ammunition or magazines and have the bolt or breech fully open when approaching a hut. This is critical for everybody's safety in the bush, regardless of how tired, wet or cold you may be from the hunt.

Always let others know where you will be hunting and when you expect to be home or back at the hut. If as a group you decide to hunt specific areas, then stick to the plan. Under no circumstances should you change your hunting area by moving onto someone else's. This is a recipe for disaster.

Make sure you are well away from any roads.

Make a note of the make, model, serial

number, action and calibre of your firearms in case they are ever mislaid or stolen. The New Zealand Police will record this information on your firearms licence record if you wish.

These are the seven golden rules, as laid out in the excellent *Arms Code — Firearms Safety Manual*.

1. Always treat every firearm as loaded until you've checked its status. It is the main responsibility of the person handing the gun to someone else to have the gun **unloaded and not cocked**. Mistakes can be made, however, so the person receiving the gun should treat it as loaded and double-check as well as ask the passer to check that the gun isn't loaded. This is critical at all times, especially when crossing a fence.

2. Never point a firearm at another person even if unloaded. When out hunting with others, the front person walking through the bush is the only person with a firearm at the ready. Others behind should have their rifles shouldered and unloaded. When getting in and out of vehicles, the firearm must remain unloaded. When transporting firearms, they are best kept in gun covers and must be secured when arriving home by placing them immediately (after cleaning) into the gun safe or gun rack and locked away. Trigger locks can also be used; these are an added precaution in case of theft or someone without permission getting their hands on the gun!

3. When hunting in a group, the gun should only be loaded by the person in the lead and only when you reach your actual hunting area and are ready to fire. It is important that those following behind adhere to this rule, and it's good practice to all clearly say as you are doing it, 'Bolt closed — no round in the chamber!' and show a mate that you have done it. It only takes seconds to do this, and will reassure everyone, especially the leader — there is nothing quite so worrying as that prickly feeling between your shoulder blades when you aren't confident that every hunter is being as careful as they need to be.

4. Identify the target beyond all doubt before firing. A tip here is to get good optics — binoculars and a good scope —

but the rule is: 'When in doubt, leave it out!' It should never happen, but hunters are shot nearly every year by poor hunters who do not follow this rule. As a responsible hunter, you should be making every effort to get as close to your quarry as possible, to reduce the chance of misidentification, and also give you a better chance at that all-important one-shot kill. Firing at great distances is for shooters, not hunters, and needs to be done by experts who spend many hours on the range. So get in close, clearly identify your target and make sure of that shot. Wounding an animal and not being able to secure it is distressing and unforgivable if you haven't been patient, practised your shooting, been determined to place that shot carefully, and moved in as close as you can to the target.

5. Ensure your firing zone is safe. This means not discharging the gun when there is a risk that the shot ricochets off rocks or water. It also means checking out the background behind the quarry. Remember, a bullet can travel great distances and gradually loops in a curve as it loses energy. So shooting at a hare sitting on top of a low hill above you could result in the bullet curving well past the target and down into farmland making it incredibly dangerous for stock or other people. A safe background to fire a gun at is a background where, with all due care, there is very little if any likelihood of a bullet missing the target and going on to hit an unintended target, such as farm animals or another human being. A farm hillside is an example of a perfect background where a bullet can pass through an animal and into the bank harmlessly. Hunters need to be aware that bullets can hit the target but still pass through and have the power to injure or kill afterwards. If spotlighting, only ever have one gun on the go. The excitement of the hunt, spotting animals to shoot and the pitch-darkness can mean a hunting party with multiple guns doesn't always know where the gun holder is. This situation becomes even more dangerous when a possibly wounded animal is chased in order to dispatch it and people lose track of exactly what is going on. This is highly dangerous, so one gun is the name of the game.

6. All guns should be stored safely, and preferably with the ammunition locked away securely elsewhere in case of burglary. Always make the gun safe by removing the bolt, ammunition and any magazine, and opening the breech (where the bullets go) so that it is easier to see that it is unloaded before storing it away in the car or at home.

7. No alcohol or drugs when handling firearms. The law is quite clear and the two don't mix. Don't hunt with anyone who has been drinking or taken drugs.

CARE OF FIREARMS

A basic cleaning kit for all rifles should contain a string pull-through matched to the calibre of the rifle, a bronze brush also matched to the calibre of the rifle, rifle oil (which is a preservative), flannelette cloth patches approximately 5 by 10 centimetres, a cleaning rod and a jag also to suit the calibre. If the rifle has a wooden stock, then boiled linseed oil is all that you need.

Get to know the workings of your gun, preferably with guidance early on, and how to clean it carefully. If the adults you are with are unsure, your local hunting/fishing store should be able to guide you.

RABBIT AND HARE HUNTING

So, you're keen to hunt rabbits or hares? Here are some basics that will safely add to your fun in the outdoors and greatly increase your chance of success.

BEFORE YOU HUNT

The type of gun you use for rabbit and hare hunting is very important, as there is a big difference between an air rifle's power and a .22 **calibre**.

Most budding hunters begin their careers with the humble air rifle, which is a great starting point as they don't require the owner to be a licensed firearms holder, so long as they are supervised by a person 18 years or older. (To use an air rifle unsupervised, you must be 18 years or older or aged 16 or 17 and hold a licence.)

An air gun is any weapon that has a gas or compressed air firing mechanism, including air rifles, air pistols, BB guns, soft air pellet guns and paintball guns. The more power you have, the greater the distance you can safely shoot at a target and get a clean kill.

Some air rifles are now immensely powerful, capable of nailing a rabbit out to 50 metres, so they always need to be treated with respect. The habits formed here will serve you well into the future: good habits = plenty of rabbits! The next step could be a .22 calibre — also great fun and relatively cheap. Befriend your local sports store owner and pick their brains over selection and price. Ensure that you go through the licence process, not just to gain the licence but also to learn as much as possible.

The first step is to get to know what your gun can do at still targets drawn on paper or cardboard. Find a safe place to fire your gun, thinking especially of one of the main target rules — **have a safe background**. A bullet can travel a long way after going through a target, so make sure your backdrop will stop the bullet or pellet. Joining a club will give you access to a range where you can practise.

The key to good shooting is putting in the practice so you can place that shot exactly where you want it. Regularly hitting the target is your first goal, followed by adding some more distance as you get more accurate. Keeping a journal to record your progress makes interesting reading!

Once you are proficient with an air rifle on targets, consistently and accurately hitting what you are aiming at, a move to live game will be far more successful.

BASIC BALLISTICS

Put simply, **guns have the power to kill**. Therefore it's important for every hunter to understand some basic **ballistics**.

The bullet or projectile is what flies out of the barrel, heading in the direction the gun was pointing at. The casing contains the gunpowder which provides the propulsion behind the bullet. The bigger the casing, the more gunpowder, the further the bullet can travel and therefore hit or kill the target.

In nearly all ammunition the casing is made out of brass and holds another vital component, the primer, which is at the very base of the casing. When the trigger is squeezed, the firing pin whacks into the primer, creating an instant ignition of the primer and gunpowder. Once that bullet is on its way down the barrel, there is no stopping it.

A hunting bullet or projectile is designed to expand on impact in order to achieve as much damage as possible to ensure a quick kill. So it had better be aimed at the intended target. **There are no second chances.**

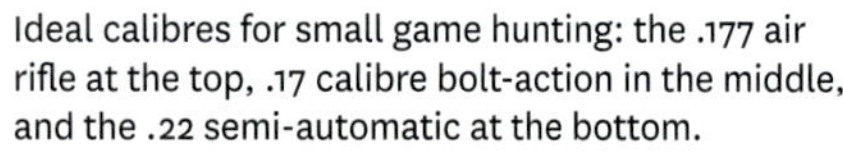

Ideal calibres for small game hunting: the .177 air rifle at the top, .17 calibre bolt-action in the middle, and the .22 semi-automatic at the bottom.

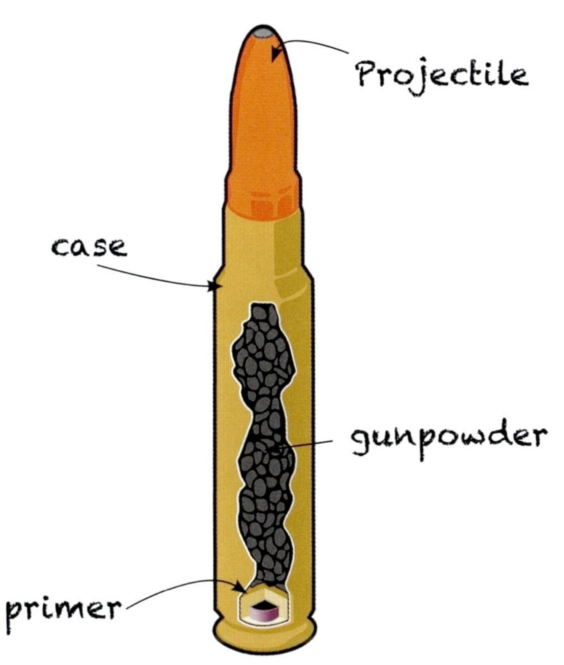

WHERE TO HUNT

Rabbits love short grass and low bushy cover to run into when they are scared. So creek and river beds are top spots to hunt. Always ask permission of the landowner before walking onto their land, and check with them to see if there are any other hunters on their land or in the area. Sheep farms are better than dairy farms for rabbit hunting as they generally have shorter grass — and these critters don't like getting wet moving through the grass. Farmland with low hills gives you a chance to try for longer shots with a .22. Hares have longer ears and are much larger than a rabbit, sometimes two-and-a-half times a rabbit's weight. The ears on a hare are also black-tipped, which is highly distinctive in the field. Hares are built for speed and have much longer legs than a rabbit — and when eaten have a stronger flavour. Hares will shape their home, called a 'form', under logs or the base of a tree, or in tight, long grass, while rabbits dig out elaborate holes or 'burrows'. Hares seem to prefer the longer grass found on dairy farms.

SIGNS TO LOOK FOR

Along the edges of fence lines, where there is heavy cover on one side and grass on the other, are good areas to look for rabbit runs. Runs are well-worn pathways in the grass that rabbits use to travel to their feeding areas. They will push through the same place under the bottom wire. These are their escape routes, so remember these spots the next time you are out hunting, and approach the area carefully as 'Brer Rabbit' is likely to be out and about. Other obvious signs are diggings and rabbit poo or droppings.

These areas are really good just before the light goes at early evening as the animals are often further away from cover. Hares, especially, nestle in for a sleep in 'beds' — they will often crouch down as you get nearer and then give you a heck of a fright by exploding out right from under your feet.

When there are plenty of rabbits, the grass will be eaten down quite a lot near their runs compared to surrounding grass levels.

A well-behaved hunting dog can be used to flush out rabbits in light cover. There is nothing more exciting than when your dog stops and points to a hidden rabbit or hare in long grass. Before pulling the trigger you must be extra careful that your dog is not in the line of fire or is in danger of a **ricochet**. A missed opportunity to fire your gun is far better than injuring your dog or worse. In scrubby cover, a dog is often the only way of finding a wounded animal which you need to make sure is caught quickly.

HOW TO HUNT

Once you have an area in which to hunt, the best times of the day for rabbits and hares are early in the morning and late afternoon to early evening. Always try to hunt into the wind as all game animals have a keen sense of smell, and if they smell you they will be long gone before you get anywhere near them. Also try to hunt with the sun at your back, as low sun can work very well for you. The sun will be in the eyes of the rabbits or hares — both of which have excellent eyesight and hearing — and you will be effectively in shadow.

Make sure you use every bit of cover when stalking in close. Stop often when you are hunting to look closely ahead for game and to plan out where you are going to stalk using cover. Bush fence lines and drains are good methods of breaking your outline, and they allow you to move closer to the target. Bush edges, in particular, must be hunted properly. Do not hunt by remaining out in the open simply because it is easier to cover ground. Check out spots in the distance and nip into the bush, moving very slowly, and while in the shade and cover come slowly out to the last few trees, moving and stopping irregularly just as an animal would.

Hunting rabbits in farmlet areas, which are particularly prevalent in New Zealand, is ideal. It's better to use air rifles in these areas as they do not make loud bangs like firearms do, and as long as you follow all the usual safety rules then there are plenty of bunnies to go for. Often outbuildings and barns can provide cover for the hunter and escape routes for rabbits as they scurry away from hawks or dogs. Rabbit numbers can skyrocket when grass cover is being kept down, which rabbits prefer especially when wet, and when there is less pressure from guns because of close neighbours.

A pair of binoculars can help for long-

range shooting with a more powerful gun. Look closely for shapes in the shadows, as these can be really hard to spot if you are on the move all the time. Sounds such as talking and metal clinking together will have the rabbits running for cover.

The key to successfully killing a game animal is to get close enough to place that all-important one shot. So in stalking you are always thinking of ways to check out a likely patch while staying largely hidden behind low scrub. Mistakes made in stalking rabbits or hares when they see, hear or smell you need to be remembered and avoided the next time out hunting.

It is not recommended that you shoot at a running animal with a rifle — this is best left to an expert or if you are hunting with a shotgun as that is what it is designed for. A shotgun shoots many small pellets and has a greater chance of killing running game at short distances.

USING A SCOPE

While open sights are a good start for a beginner, you can take accuracy to another level by putting a low-powered **scope** onto the air rifle. You have a choice of **recticles**. Your eye will focus quickly enough on any of the styles with plenty of practice. The power of the scope is also up to you and the distances you think you will mostly be shooting at. A standard 4x power scope is hard to beat. A 4x power scope magnifies what the hunter sees by four times. If you want more flexibility then a 3x to 9x vari-power is excellent. You can keep the scope on 3x power while hunting, and if

a hare is spotted at a decent distance then you can crank up the scope's power to 9x which brings your target that much closer, making it easier to shoot.

Be very careful with scopes, though, as they can narrow your field of vision. This means you can be so focused on what is in your scope that you don't see around the target, and another person out hunting in the same area may move too close to your target just as you fire. The top dial adjusts the horizontal recticle up or down, while the side dial adjusts the vertical recticle, moving it sideways right or left.

To sight in your rifle it pays to fire three or four shots at a target from a close distance of around 25 metres. The pattern of bullet holes will indicate which dials you need to adjust. Then fire off three more rounds at the same distance and check whether your adjustments were enough.

Next, increase the distance to about 40 to 50 metres and go through the same process. At greater distances, especially with an air rifle or .22, there will be some bullet drop as the bullet loses power, so sight in your rifle to the most likely distances at which you can regularly hit a target comfortably and therefore achieve clean, one-shot kills.

Tip:
Always place the rifle onto a padded sack or a bag, as shown in the photo to the left, to ensure the rifle doesn't move as you place your shots.

SPOTLIGHTING

Spotlighting can be a huge amount of fun if done properly. But there should only ever be one gun used because of the risk in the dark. As with all hunting, it is important that you hunt with someone else who is experienced in this form of hunting. There are two things you will need to be aware of:

1. Trying to work out how far away game is can be more difficult.
2. It is especially important to be extra careful when choosing the background to your shot.

A torch, headlamp or, better still, a proper spotlight has the power to freeze a rabbit or hare giving you a steady shot. What to look for are those pink glowing eyes in the beam of light — a sure sign that it is what you are after — but you must make sure of the target before firing.

Note that you can't spotlight on Department of Conservation (DOC) land, and you must have permission from the landowner to spotlight.

HOW TO SKIN YOUR RABBIT

1. Cut the skin around each of the back legs.
2. Place the knife on the inside of each leg between the skin and leg, then make a cut across the body and up to the end of the other back leg.
3. Use both hands to push up from the stomach to the rib area, peeling the skin away from the body.
4. Cut up the cleared skin, peeling away as you go, until you reach the chin.
5. Then cut across the inside of each front leg right to the end.
6. Now, holding the skin edge near the middle of the rabbit, use one hand to push, and peel with the other hand until you free up the skin towards the backbone on one side. Then repeat from the other side until you can place your boot across the backbone, between the freed-up skin and the rabbit.
7. Pull up on the skin towards the back legs, firmly treading down with your boot until the back legs are freed of skin. You may need to prise with your thumb or knuckles so both legs will give up their hold on the skin.
8. Time now to repeat on the front legs and pull up hard onto the skin, holding the head.
9. Once the skin has reached the base of the ears, you can cut across at this point as it is very fiddly to try to skin out a head. You will be left with a standard animal skin shape that is typical of even the largest game animal.

A simple mix of baking soda and **kerosene** or egg and hot water mixed into a paste will cure the skin and keep flies off it as long as you haven't left any stray meat attached. Hang the skin up high, well away from your dog or cat, and it will be ready in a week.

A RECIPE TO TRY

RABBIT NUGGETS

INGREDIENTS

rabbit fillets

2 eggs

a handful of breadcrumbs

a handful of Diamond Coat'n Cook

good-quality olive oil

METHOD

1. Cut down the spine of the animal, just to the right and left of the backbone, and then fillet in against the ribs towards the spine. This will give you a long strip of meat just as with a deer. There is good meat also on the back legs, but too little on the front so don't bother with these. Hold the back leg and make a cut right up near the base of the leg near the tail. Cut across the top of the hamstring to the bone, pulling and carefully cutting as the meat starts to come away from the bone. This is a feel thing, so just make sure you always cut away from your fingers and that the blade is sharp — there are more accidents with blunt knives forcing the cuts!
2. Cut across the grain into 1 cm thick medallions/chunks, making sure you have taken off any silver skin. Beat 2 eggs in a bowl, mix in meat.
3. In a plastic bag, mix together the breadcrumbs and Coat'n Cook.
4. Add the meat to the mix, shaking the ingredients carefully.
5. Cook in a pan with olive oil until both sides are golden brown. These go great with dipping sauces.

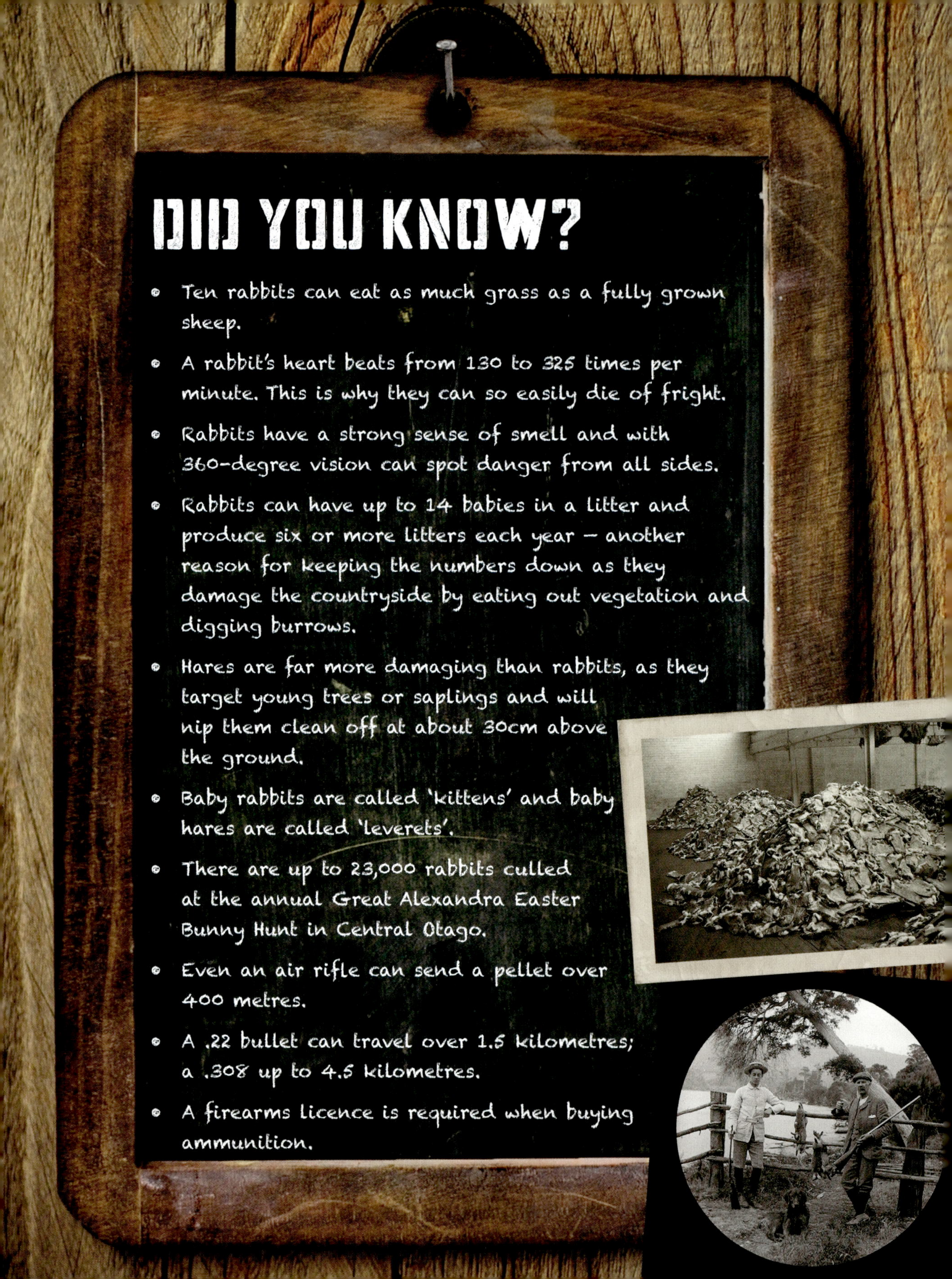

DID YOU KNOW?

- Ten rabbits can eat as much grass as a fully grown sheep.
- A rabbit's heart beats from 130 to 325 times per minute. This is why they can so easily die of fright.
- Rabbits have a strong sense of smell and with 360-degree vision can spot danger from all sides.
- Rabbits can have up to 14 babies in a litter and produce six or more litters each year – another reason for keeping the numbers down as they damage the countryside by eating out vegetation and digging burrows.
- Hares are far more damaging than rabbits, as they target young trees or saplings and will nip them clean off at about 30cm above the ground.
- Baby rabbits are called 'kittens' and baby hares are called 'leverets'.
- There are up to 23,000 rabbits culled at the annual Great Alexandra Easter Bunny Hunt in Central Otago.
- Even an air rifle can send a pellet over 400 metres.
- A .22 bullet can travel over 1.5 kilometres; a .308 up to 4.5 kilometres.
- A firearms licence is required when buying ammunition.

GLOSSARY

Ballistics The study of how firearms work, including the firing, flight and effects of ammunition.

Calibre The size and power of a rifle bullet.

Cocked A firearm is considered cocked when there is a bullet in the breech and the hunter only has to release the safety catch, the small switch placed near the bolt side of the gun, then pull the trigger for the gun to fire.

Kerosene A fuel just like petrol.

Recticle Refers to the intersecting lines in the shape of a cross. Sometimes called 'cross hairs'.

Ricochet Where a bullet can bounce off a surface and still keep on going.

Scope A rifle sight capable of magnifying the target so it looks closer. 'Scope' is the shortened word for telescope or common usage for 'rifle scope'.

DUCK AND GOOSE HUNTING

To bring a game bird to the ground, you need to practise and prepare. However, unlike rifle shooting where placing a single bullet into a target can be practised and achieved reasonably easily, to shoot game birds in mid-air – which you must do legally – you have to use a shotgun.

BEFORE YOU HUNT

A shotgun is designed to send out a shot charge of pellets much like a handful of gravel, which creates a spread, giving the hunter a greater chance of striking the target. The shotgun shell is similar to the rifle bullet in that there is a primer located at the base of the **cartridge** and gunpowder sits above the primer ready to propel lots of lead or steel pellets down the barrel. The pellets are held in a protective plastic wad, which is designed to protect the barrel, and ensures a better killing pattern.

One of the quickest ways to see just what shells do in your gun is to fire at large sheets of paper from various distances, such as 20 metres right out to 50 metres. You will be surprised at how big the gaps are on the sheet the further away the target is. This should give you an idea of the sort

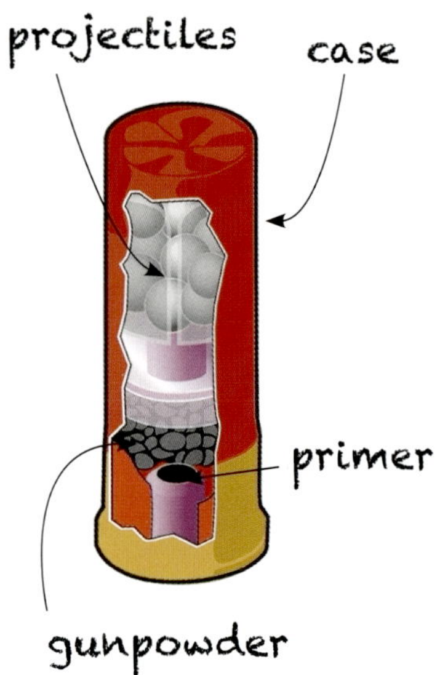

1. A common .12 gauge semi-automatic shotgun.
2. A camouflaged light .20 gauge, great for close-range hunting.
3. A single-shot .410, also for shooting at close range.
4. A combination .410 gauge shotgun with a .22 rifle barrel on top.

of distances from which you should be shooting at ducks or geese. The pellets also start to lose their power and therefore ability to penetrate and kill your quarry. Poor hunters 'sky bust' at distant, out-of-range targets — make sure you are not one of those, as no one likes wounding animals.

Pellets can be bought in different sizes. Rabbits, magpies, rats or ducks can be killed with smaller pellets as they create dense patterns at short distances, but once out to 30 metres-plus, larger pellets are a must to penetrate a bird's feathers. When shooting over a waterway the law now states that hunters need to use steel shot, as this is less toxic on the environment. Water birds, searching for weed and snails, might ingest or swallow lead pellets which have sunk to the bottom of the waterways — lead is poisonous and can kill birds. Steel doesn't maintain its killing power as well as lead, so hunters have to use larger-sized pellets. As a guide, anything from BB through to number 4 shot in steel is required for ducks and geese. Rabbits can be shot with lead, and number 6 through to 4 shot is deadly out to 30 to 45 metres. It is easy to imagine that these little pellets are

A shotgun will only fire when the breech is closed.

relatively harmless, but in fact at very close range they can cause massive damage and kill humans. While it would be hard to imagine that a pellet or two striking a human at a range of 50 plus metres would kill them, **a shotgun in any calibre at close range is lethal**.

A .410 or .20 gauge gun are excellent calibres to start with, as the **recoil** from the shot is more manageable and will lessen the habit of flinching, which is when the shooter squints and moves with imaginary recoil. Sometimes this even happens just before the trigger is squeezed, which leads to the gun aim being pulled away from the target. Either .410 or .20 gauge guns are effective between anything from 15 to 35 metres; .12 gauge has a wider window going out to 45 metres depending on the shot size used. 12 gauge shot shells can be bought in 3½ inch cartridges right down to 2¾ inch shells and in pellet sizes from a single slug for large game right down to number 8 or 9 for clay-bird target shooting. For general duck hunting, use 2¾ shells in 2, 3 or 4 steel shot. If you are shooting in fields away from water, then lead shot can be used and, because they hit harder due to lead being heavier than steel, pellet size can be brought out to 5s and 6s. An added advantage is more pellets striking the bird, resulting in cleaner kills.

A beginner should use a more open **choke** because it increases the chance of getting a hit, and these can be screwed in, or set in an older gun. Being able to change the choke means you can control the spread of the pellets. As mentioned above, you need to know what your gun and ammo is capable of by shooting at large sheets of paper at different distances.

If it is clay-bird or target shooting you enjoy, then a cheap option for all the family is to buy a hand thrower, a box of clays and ammo. Even better still, join a gun club and learn proper footwork, gun handling and all the necessary safety aspects from the experts. As you get better and better, there are handicap systems which move you gradually further and further away from the trap (where the clays are released).

WHEN TO HUNT

Duck hunting can be as simple or complicated as you make it. The thing to remember is that, unlike rabbit shooting, there is only a certain time of the year when ducks can be legally hunted. This is between 6.30 a.m. and 6.30 p.m. from the first weekend in May, generally through to the end of June. There are different season lengths in different parts of New Zealand, and summer crop shooting can be available. Your local Fish & Game office will set you right here.

WHERE TO HUNT

Ducks love company, so will naturally look to land where other ducks are. They also love their food, so areas where they can eat, such as fields of farm crops, or swamps where they can tuck into water snails, worms and seeds, are where they will be looking to land. If it is during the day, then they may simply be seeking out a safe place to rest up. Usually they will look to feed at night or late afternoon. Quiet backwaters next to very small creeks or even large rivers are excellent spots. They like a pond with some cover from hawks and humans, but if they haven't been shot at or disturbed, then even open farm stock

duck hunting blind

ponds can hold large numbers of birds just for that resting-up period during the day, so keep an eye out.

Always ask permission from the landowner/farmer before searching out these spots. You can give farmers a call, but talking to them personally is better, as they can get to know you, and explain their boundary fences and other considerations special to their place. Listen carefully and always leave farm gates as you find them. Make a mistake with anything here and you could be ruining a great hunting spot for yourself in the future and possibly endangering yourself or a hunting buddy.

Generally, you are looking for water. So a trip into the local regional council for maps will indicate waterways and access points to hunt. Public land near lakes is ideal. Local Fish & Game offices will be only too ready to help you find hunting spots. They will also know where and what the ducks are up to at that time of the year. Look for feathers at the edges of waterways, as these are a clue that ducks are using the area to **preen** themselves.

clay bird shooter

HOW TO HUNT

Traditionally, ducks are hunted from a maimai or blind. These are shelters built by hunters to keep them hidden from the ducks as they fly into your decoys (see page 35) or past your spot. Alternatively, stalking a stream or river bank and having them explode out from under the bank by your feet can set your heart racing as you swing onto the first target. Standing in the dark by a shallow puddle in the middle of a farm field hearing the chuckle feed call and whistle of approaching wings will have you straining ears and eyes to pick up the first movement.

In high winds, finding a spot where the birds are flying low as they check out calm water can be deadly. This is called pass-shooting. It takes discipline to swing past birds and judge when to let the round go once you are in front of your target. It is so easy to swing and stop the barrels as you fire, and when this is combined with strong wind the shot charge can be even further behind the intended target.

There is also nothing quite like having a large number of decoys on a big body of water such as a lake, then calling in ducks from a distance and watching their progress as they negotiate the wind and make a beeline for your decoy spread. As the whispered call goes up in the maimai to stand and shoot, the ducks or geese have their landing gear out with wings flared and feet spread. Fire!

CLOTHING

Ducks have excellent eyesight, so it is important that you wear clothing that blends in with the vegetation and areas where you are hunting. Camouflage patterns help break the human outline which can be quite a giveaway, especially later in a season when the ducks have been shot at and scared by other hunters. Camouflage patterns can take the form of splotches of at least three different shades of green or brown. They can also be even more cunning with actual branch/leaf patterns for forest hunting or swamp colourings with reed textures.

Or you can wear anything from mid- to dark green or brown, but keep away from bright colours or shiny material as the birds will spot you long before you see them — all you will hear is that raucous quack-quack as they fly off well out of range if you are stalking waterways.

Tip:
Remember that even with the best camouflage and face paint, if you are moving you will be spotted by the ducks from terrific distances.

DECOYS AND CALLING

If a spot where you have set out decoys looks great, then ducks will check it out by flying closer and closer until they are either happy enough to land or will flare off if something doesn't quite look or feel right. You can wait until they are in range to have a go at them or, when they have landed, stand and shoot them as they take off. **Remember that they cannot be shot at unless they are flying.** It is an offence to break this rule and can lead to loss of your firearm and a fine.

Generally, the more decoys you can set, the more effective they will be in getting ducks close enough to shoot. Later in the season when the ducks are extremely wary, often a single decoy or two is enough and they will zoom in straight away.

You can have a lot of fun making your own decoys out of polystyrene. Always use non-reflective paint. The more you can make the setting look natural, the more success you will have.

The rule of thumb for calling is to call little and often. Don't overdo it as this can put the ducks off coming in. There are various calls you can practise or select from with electronic callers.

Welcome call: **Q—U—A—C--K!!** Q-u-a-c-k q-u-a-c-k q-u-a-c-k q-u-a-c-k.

Come back call: **Q—U--A—C--K! Q—U—A—C—K! Q—U—A—C—K!** quack quack quack quack.

Feeding call: A soft chattering alternating ticker, ticker, ticker . . . quack, ticker, ticker . . . quack.

The feeding call is blown softly creating the 'ticker' chuckle. You need to bring your tongue up to the roof of your mouth and utter a 'tooka tooka' sound with the occasional muted quack. With practice and listening to a mob of ducks feeding, you will get better, bringing closer those ducks keen for company and tucker!

duck and goose callers

STALKING DUCKS

The key with stalking is to surprise the birds, and you are not going to do that if they see you before you can see them or get close enough for a shot. Try to keep the sun at your back and the wind in your face. Ducks can also smell you coming, and, even more importantly, any unwanted noise (even a panting dog) will carry further near water, alerting the birds — they will often start to paddle out from the bank or resting spot and be on code red, ready to depart before you can get in close enough.

Your shadow can also be a problem. Walk straight at a tree or scrub, keeping your shadow lined on this vegetation until you are close enough to shift into a gap and step forward, gun at the ready. Otherwise your shadow will cast out over the water long before you reach a shooting spot.

When ducks explode right from under your feet on the edge of a waterway with tremendous quacking, flapping and splashing, it is important that you don't panic and rush your shots. Wait to identify that they are in fact ducks you are allowed to shoot and not a teal. (The grey teal, the scaup or black teal, and the blue duck or whio are all protected and therefore not hunted in New Zealand.) This will allow the birds time to fly out to a good distance for your shot spread, and for your feet to be set at a good angle to flow through the swing, aiming for the front of the bird.

Your hunting companions, dog and farm stock are your main concern as you slip that safety catch off ready to pull the trigger. **Always be aware of where your barrels are pointing as you stalk with hunting buddies.**

USE OF DOGS

Gun dogs are the single best accessory to your hunting — full stop. A dog has terrific ability with its nose and swimming to retrieve shot ducks, and to find and then flush out ducks, which may have otherwise stayed put as hunters walk by, from the edges of waterways. There is no greater satisfaction than seeing your dog set off in the near-dark to retrieve a duck which has fallen, and then minutes later reappear with the bird in its mouth.

If you don't have a dog, then you need to be hunting with someone who does, as even with care and accuracy there will be times when you need to catch and dispatch a wounded animal as soon as possible. This brings hunter and dog close together as partners, and, if the bird is wounded, it means you have done the right thing in making sure your **quarry** doesn't suffer.

Just about any breed of dog will retrieve for you with a little practice done often, especially at the puppy stage. Outside of the May–June hunting season when you can't hunt ducks is when you can work on getting your dog — your hunting buddy — up to speed.

There are six main commands or rules your dog needs to understand:

1. **'Sit!'** Your dog must sit at your command and wait for your next instruction. With the puppy on a lead, lean towards it splaying your hand out and moving it down towards the dog's face, saying 'Sit!' firmly. The combination of command and the hand coming down will result in the pup sitting, and after a while just the command will do.

2. **'Stay!'** All dogs must stay where you command them to — especially in the back of a car just as you are opening the door. Many a dog has been hit by a vehicle when making an out-of-control exit from a car. Better still, tie them up with a lead so you control the exit.

3. **'Fetch!'** Train the dog to bring back the dummy or animal at your command. Put them on a long lead so you can reel them in, and always use an encouraging voice. As soon as they complete the retrieve, make sure you heap on the praise by patting and rubbing their tummy, and then, once they sit, carefully reward with a small bit of food. Always have them nuzzle in softly, gently taking the food, as throwing it leads to snappy dogs. Remember that you are after a soft-mouthed dog that will bring back to you the most delicate of birds such as quail.

4. **No barking.** Unless of course this is what you want them to do as with a farm dog moving stock.

5. **Direction commands.** This can take extra practice, but is all common sense and with experience greatly helps you get a duck. Set up scenarios where the retrieving dummy is hidden, and control the dog by having it on a long lead, commanding 'Stay!' and then, using your whole arm, point in the direction of the dummy and encourage the dog to move there with 'Fetch!' Use 'Stay!' if the dog is heading in the wrong direction, and then encouraging words like 'Good dog!' increasing the excitement in your voice as they get closer, just like playing a game of Hot and Cold.

6. **Walking on a lead or choker chain.** This is important to keep control over the dog and to make it respect your commands. 'Heel!' should be used whenever the dog pulls too much or simply needs to come in close to your side. Having a dog tied to your belt for use in the bush could be your aim. Absolute control can be achieved with a little practice done often. Always make a game of it.

WHAT BREEDS?

Labradors and retrievers are incredibly versatile, easy to train, make great family pets and love cold water. They can also be taught to point out quarry. Chesapeake Bay retrievers are larger breeds and very strong dogs. Any of the spaniels will work extremely hard for you and also love water. English and German short-haired pointers don't like the cold too much but are highly efficient movers on land and retrieve well. The Weimaraner is very similar to the pointers and will in fact point over **coveys** of quail or a rabbit set to spring, and swim well for water retrieves. Any of these breeds will be successful for you as long as you put in the time and are patient with them.
Dogs can retrieve underwater as well.

DID YOU KNOW?

- Dogs can detect a scent trail on water.
- You are only allowed to use steel shot pellets over larger bodies of water. Make sure you check out the regulations when you buy your licence in the accompanying Fish & Game booklet.
- Ducks and geese can hear you calling more than 500 metres away, depending on the wind direction.
- Depending on the pellet size and charge behind it, a shotgun pellet can cover from 200 to 750 metres.
- Shotgun target shooting is an Olympic sport.

GLOSSARY

Cartridge The full shell casing with primer, gunpowder and bullet or pellets assembled.

Choke The constriction at the end of the barrel which controls the spread of pellets.

Preen When a bird cleans or smoothes its feathers with its beak or bill.

Quarry The game you are hunting.

Recoil The kick a gun delivers as the shot is taken.

MAGPIES, STARLINGS AND OTHER PESTS

Magpies are the black-and-white bandits of New Zealand's skies. In the spring they become very territorial and will dive-bomb anything coming close to their nest. They are especially dangerous to cyclists, golfers and children walking home from school. So their numbers need reducing at times. Shooting them can be tricky, as they learn fast if you miss a shot. They can also be trapped and moved to another area if you do not want to kill them.

BEFORE YOU HUNT

A rifle or shotgun in a variety of calibres used at the right distances can be effective in reducing magpie numbers. Remember, as always, the importance of safety and ensuring a clean, one-shot kill. Know the gun you are going to use and what it is capable of, as magpies can be tough creatures and it takes a well-placed shot from a rifle to be successful. It's also important to remember that a shotgun is the only firearm suitable for shooting at birds in flight.

Air rifles can kill out to 25 metres, but this is getting up to their full range. The .22 or .17 is ideal for stalking magpies as they can be effective out to 90 to 100 metres

consistently — but that target area is getting mighty small unless you have a well-sighted scope set up with your rifle. The advantages of open sights are that they are sturdy, cheap, reasonably quick to learn to use after practice in aiming at a target, and don't tend to mist up in heavy rain. They also allow peripheral vision. Their disadvantages are that, when aligning with the target, the shooter has to consider both sights and the target, whereas with a telescopic sight it is just cross hairs and target. The scope is also far more precise and is adjustable, with elevation and sideways corrections.

A shotgun in any calibre from .410, .16, .20 or .12 gauges works well at close range on anything from 15 to 40 metres.

The many pellets in a shotgun cartridge increase the chance of getting a quick, clean kill. Cartridges can be bought in many sizes.

If the bird is really close, then anything from number 9 to number 7 will do what's needed, but if the distance is further, say 25 metres, for anything less than a .20 gauge then number 6 through to number 4 are effective. Refer back to pages 30–31 for more on shotgun shells.

As with the rifle, you need to know what your shotgun can do from a variety of distances. Set up a safe area with several large sheets of paper or cardboard. Draw a single target, and then try at distances of 10 metres through to 30 metres, and work out the range from which you can regularly hit the centre before having a go at a magpie. You will be surprised at how quickly the spread of pellets widens: the bigger the gap, the more chance of missing or wounding the bird.

As pellets travel in a stream shape, the best way to see this is to safely shoot at a floating target on a still piece of water. As you gradually move further away with each shot, the stream of pellets will lengthen.

WHERE TO HUNT

Make sure you are well away from any roads. The trick is to get the birds close enough, and that requires either attracting them to you or being in a spot where they are flying in. Finding where magpies are nesting, and waiting until they fly up to or from the nest, works well, especially at times when they are very **territorial** and quick to swoop.

If your chooks are being swooped on, then put yourself near the chicken coop and wait for the action. This works well if you place the chook food where the chickens will feed, and gives you a close shot on the magpie as it dive-bombs in.

If you are not in a position to use a firearm, contact your local branch of Forest & Bird or regional council office. They will either destroy the birds or relocate them elsewhere in live capture traps.

HOW TO HUNT

It is important that you study your quarry and can distinguish it from other birds. A blackbird and a starling can be mixed up in poor light at early morning or evening, so you also need to take note of their flight patterns in the air. A starling will beat its wings fast and pause before starting up again, so its flight is a series of loops, whereas a blackbird will swerve through vegetation. While blackbirds are a nuisance in the vege garden, it is the starling which we have far too many of and which carries disease. The .20 gauge, .16 or even .410 are ideal calibres to be using.

Make enquiries around the end of summer at any local vineyards, and olive groves later in autumn. You will be surprised at how many will be only too glad to have their starling populations stirred up. A number of them

will be employing automatic bird scarers, kites resembling hawks (which are predators of starlings), and kill tables dotted around their property where dead rabbit or sheep heads are placed 2 to 3 metres above the ground to attract the hawks in.

At certain times of the year, bird numbers will increase and the pressure on gathering home-grown fruit and getting it to the kitchen undamaged can become a problem. The careers of many up-and-coming young hunters have been forged in stalks and shots at birds in the garden with an air rifle. Why not ask your parents or neighbours for small bounty payments and make some pocket money by doing a good deed?

OTHER PESTS

RATS

Given the conservation effort to reduce rat numbers and safeguard more native bird chicks through to adulthood, let's just say these critters are well and truly fair game!

Air rifles are highly effective, but you need to set up your field of fire by placing food to attract rats within range and your shooting ability. So get comfortable where the rats can't see you, no more than 10 metres away, and downwind so they can't smell you. Place a small amount of the food behind a barn or chook house near where they come out, and a large amount right where you want to nail them.

An even better option is 'rat shot' — a .22 cartridge designed to shoot number 10 lead shot pellets at close range at birds or rats inside barns — which was originally designed to deal with snakes in the United States. A distance gauge would be anything from 3 to 8 metres for an effective killing range.

A leg-hold trap set in a pipe or bait station also works really well on rats. Any food for bait will attract them. Siting the trap next to a back wall or along a fence line are ideal spots, as rats will travel along these pathways because they provide cover and a ready means of escape. A rat will travel along a pipe to get to where it wants to go without having to move away from its natural highway.

FERRETS, STOATS AND WEASELS [MUSTELID FAMILY]

These three 'mustelid musketeers' are the scourge of native birdlife and domestic poultry. They are born killers that, unlike so many other hunter carnivores, will not stop killing even when they have had enough to eat. They can destroy a whole nest full of fledgling native birds in one night as they are great climbers; or make an easier meal of ducklings just before they are capable of flying.

Introduced into New Zealand in the 1870s to control rabbit numbers, mustelids very quickly adapted to far easier food sources. They are incredibly secretive and, unless you disturb them sleeping behind a pile of firewood or bales of hay during the day, the only sign of their presence will be dead animals and footprints in soft ground.

Being largely **nocturnal**, they will sleep for up to 18 hours and then cover huge distances in search of food. It is not unusual for any of these animals to range 3 to 4 kilometres from their nest.

Trapping is by far the best method of reducing mustelid numbers. There are many varieties of traps, but you will need to be careful with how the traps are set as these creatures are extremely wary of 'new' finds in their territory. Keep your scent down to a minimum by covering traps with loose grass, and, once an animal is caught, rubbing their scent over the trap will fire up the next victim to check it out. You could make use of any rats caught and killed by using them as bait. A fresh farm egg for bait works well, too, as it will not go off easily over time.

Live capture cages must have everything going for them in terms of the animal being hungry and therefore super-keen to eat: the closer to their **den**, the better. Telltale signs like feathers and other animal carcass leftovers, along with well-worn tracks leading under or into a warm, dry outbuilding or clump of toi toi, are dead giveaways. If your dog goes ballistic near the den with their hackles up, then 'Monsieur Mustelid' is in residence.

The best technique is to attach a fresh section of a dead rabbit or hare on a fence about 30 centimetres above a leg-hold trap which has been set where the animals have a worn track tunnel. They will be so engrossed in sussing out just where that lovely smell is coming from that they will walk right into the trap.

All traps must be checked daily, and first thing in the morning is the only time for leg-hold traps and even boxed stations with traps inside. The reason is that the mustelid's mate will highly likely come looking for it and you can get rid of both in under 24 hours.

Every effort needs to be made to ensure that family pets are safe from leg-hold traps. So use common sense when choosing the type of trap and how it is set. By making the entry hole into a box station small enough for your target species, a family cat will be safe.

DID YOU KNOW?

- Magpies were introduced into New Zealand in the 1860s to help control insect pests on farms. They have been known to band together in large groups of 100 or more.
- Magpies will eat anything, including insects, frogs, lizards, small birds, dying sheep and even grain. An intelligent bird, they are able to mimic other bird calls to identify where the birds are so they can attack them.
- Female ferrets are called 'jills', and males 'hobs'.

leg-hold trap

GLOSSARY

Den A mustelid (ferret, stoat or weasel) nest.

Territorial A magpie or other animal's protective behaviour of its home area.

Nocturnal Most active at night.

POSSUM HUNTING

Possum hunting is fun, safe and you are doing a really good deed by reducing the numbers of this introduced pest – plus you can make some money out of it! Possum skins can fetch as much as $16 for first-grade large skins. But if skinning and tacking the skin out on boards isn't your thing, then plucking the fur is another way of bringing in some cash – you can get up to $145 per kilogram for plucked fur.

WHERE TO HUNT

Just about anywhere in New Zealand where you can find bush or scrub, there is bound to be a possum. They can even inhabit flax swamps in coastal areas. As with any form of hunting, you need to do some research by contacting the Department of Conservation or your regional council, who will be only too happy to put you onto specific areas or tell you of farmers to contact. They will also inform you of the latest 1080 poison drop (designed to kill possums because they carry tuberculosis) and advise you where and when you can hunt. Obtaining a map from your local bookstore or the regional council will help you understand the terrain, the steepness

possum marks

possum fur

of the bush, and where those sunny north-facing slopes which possums prefer are to be found.

Going for a walk to look for **sign** is a good idea before you start hunting with traps, as it saves a lot of wasted energy, especially if there aren't many possums in residence. Possums leave clear signs once you know what to look for. Gnawing on tree trunks just off from the ground, and scratching on the trunk as they start their climb, are dead giveaways. Male possums will gnaw or chew parts of the trunk near the base to mark their territory, leaving square horizontal teeth marks.

Game trails on the forest or scrub floor and leading under boundary fences provide more proof of possum presence, along with leaves eaten off specific trees, and of course droppings. Possums will share these trails with lots of other creatures, and the fresher the poo, the more animals there will be.

Brushtail possums prefer north-facing slopes warmed up by the early-morning sun, whereas south-facing slopes can remain in shadow all day depending on the terrain. Leading ridges are prime spots to lay traps, as possums prefer uncluttered forest floor to travel along as they forage for food. Sign to look for here includes trampled-down forest leaves and smooth dirt areas forming obvious possum highways.

IDENTIFYING POISON

Of all the people going into the bush, those wanting to trap possums need to be extra careful about possible poison baits. Because you will be heading right to the spots frequented by possums, the very trees you want to set a trap on are likely to have been used at some stage by a possum hunter using poison. Possum poison line trappers use potassium cyanide, an exceedingly dangerous substance for humans (and dogs), which comes out of a tube just like green toothpaste. It will usually have scented flour placed over it to act as a lure to the possum.

If you accidentally step on a bait, simply get a stick and carefully scrape it off, covering the poison residue with dirt. **Do not ever touch it directly with your hands.** 1080 will most likely be dropped by helicopter either in carrots or as pellets. This type of poison is most toxic to your dog if it eats a poisoned possum carcass, and unless you carry an antidote with you it is likely the dog will not survive. So either keep your dog on a leash or out of areas signposted as a poison drop region. In fact, it pays to keep a small canister of dishwashing powder in your pack, for when you suspect the dog has eaten part of a poisoned carcass. Force this powder down the animal's throat to induce vomiting, and then get it to a vet as soon as possible.

Poison signs should be prominently posted at the beginnings of tracks, road ends, farm gates and even in the local newspaper. A private cyanide operator is also required to tack up signs, but you should not totally rely on this, as some prefer to keep quiet about where they are hunting even though it is potentially dangerous to others.

Brodifacoum is another poison in pellet form used largely for rats but sometimes also for possums near farmhouses or townships. If you live in a rural or semi-rural area of New Zealand, you may have seen a brochure stating clearly what laid poison looks like and how to treat it if you come across it in the bush.

HOW TO HUNT

TRAPPING

Possum trapping is usually done with a metal-jawed leg-hold trap which if set well will not only be more successful but will cause minimum stress to the animal. Remember, if you are skinning your possums you don't want to damage the skin; always set traps so that the possum can stay on the ground near the tree trunk until you kill it quickly. The best way to do this is to grab the tail and give it one good blow to the head with a hammer. A rifle can also be used, but be careful of ricochets at such close range. A head shot in close with a .22 or even a .22 short-bullet is very quick and humane.

A small section of the tree can be **blazed** just above the trap or a small piece of tinfoil tacked down to attract the inquisitive possum. Always place the trap with the trigger tongue facing the oncoming possum, as this will result in a better leg-hold catch. Sticks can be placed to guide the possum in towards the trap or a short branch wedged at a 45-degree angle against the tree. Possums naturally seek out logs to travel along, and so this method entices them to jump up onto the log, making it easier to climb the tree.

Sturdy boots covering your ankles are

recommended footwear for trapping. It also pays to wear longs to protect your legs as often the 'possumer' has to push through gorse or low scrub to get to hunting spots. Putties are even better because they cover all the lower leg area. Some hunters stitch extra material to the front and at thigh-level, as this is where you can get scratched heavily. Use a sturdy pack to hold the traps. A belt to hold your hammer or small axe, a bag of staples and flour scent are handy, too. Always throw a waterproof coat balled up into the pack just in case the weather turns.

Scent lures that trappers use include everything from vanilla or almond essence to **aniseed** and curry powder. With the possum being naturally curious, all manner of scents can be tried. Even aftershave has been recorded as having been highly effective! On moonlit nights, try tacking a small strip of tinfoil just above the trap to catch the moonlight. This can be spotted 30 to 40 metres away in the bush, so a possum will be sure to check it out.

Timms traps are used extensively by regional councils on river boundaries on farms and close to farm buildings, as domestic cats won't place their heads inside the small opening. An apple baited with aniseed or vanilla essence placed in a Timms trap will very effectively produce a quick kill. The possum places its head in the opening to eat the apple and a spring-loaded bar breaks its neck in a flash.

Cage traps are best used near outbuildings or barns, or close to farmhouses, as they can sometimes end up catching wild cats and domestic cats or other pets. These traps are much safer for these animals and easy to release them from. You should always find out if the farmer has a cat and, when in doubt, let the animal go. If it is a hissing, spitting wild cat then shoot it humanely, as they do even more damage to birdlife in native forests than possums, ferrets or stoats. Again, use an apple scented with vanilla or aniseed and place it in the cage opening where it is easy for the possum to wander in. Set the cage trap in a quiet spot away from farm dog kennels and other high-use areas, such as garages or barns, and your success rate will go up.

SPOTLIGHTING

Setting yourself up with a good spotlight makes it so much easier and safer to identify your target at night. Headlamps are good, especially the rechargeable ones, and they will save you money in the long run. Rechargeable batteries in a standard torch will work at short distances.

Finding areas where a safe hunt can take place requires planning and care. Because it is night time and the gun will be aimed up in trees, extra safety precautions are needed. **When spotlighting, there should always only be one loaded gun in use.** This is because the poor light affects your ability to see clearly — not just the target, but the surrounding area. Everyone in the hunting party needs to know the one gun is loaded **only** when in the act of shooting at the target and with the rest of the party behind the shooter.

This form of hunting can be fast and exciting, and it is so easy for one or more in the group to forget the basic rules of firearm safety as they get caught up in the action. It pays to have one member as the person in charge — usually the one with the most experience.

Plan to use daylight to check out prominent trees that may be a paddock away from the bush line, especially good if they are in a crop paddock as they can produce high numbers of possums in a small area. Sometimes these trees can resemble Christmas trees with the eyes of numerous possums reflecting back just like fairy lights. Look for these favourite communal spots when trapping. It is not uncommon to catch four or five animals from the same tree night after night.

An air rifle that can shoot at around 240 metres per second is needed to effectively kill a possum. The .22 is ideal, and it is advisable to have a scope on low power as it will make the shot even more accurate. This is important if you are going to sell the skin, as you will be going for a head shot. There are plenty of .22 or .17 calibre firearms which can have fully moderated barrels or moderators attached at the end of the barrel to lower the noise when fired. There is low-velocity .22 ammunition which further reduces shot noise. Any one of these calibres is ideal for spotlighting.

Just remember that at night it is harder to guarantee the background

air gun pellets

to your target even when you have done a daylight check, and you are shooting up into trees. Therefore you need a bullet that hits with enough power but doesn't travel through and well past the target.

A well-trained dog can greatly add to the success of the hunt, by finding and treeing possums, allowing for a shot. Any breed can be trained to do this, with smaller breeds such as the Jack Russell or fox terrier being very effective at getting into those hard-to-reach places where possums love to hide. Training your dog to bark as soon as they are onto an animal ensures the possum gets up a tree as quickly as possible and alerts you to their presence.

SKINNING OR PLUCKING THE FUR

See the 'How to skin your rabbit' section on page 24, as the same basic approach applies to possums. Once the whole skin is off and the tail is left, place one foot on the back legs and one foot on the body, twist the skin around the tail, gripping the base of the tail between your index and middle fingers, pulling up as you twist, and the tail will slip off nicely.

The only time to pluck is when the animal is still warm, as the fur is a lot harder coming off when it cools down. About 10 possums can make up to $100, and you don't have all that work skinning, tacking out on drying boards, and then brushing out ready for sale. Google 'possum fur' and you'll find a place near you to sell your skins or fur.

GLOSSARY

Aniseed An oil from the *Pimpinella anisum* herb which smells exactly like liquorice.

Blazed When a small section of bark is chipped off a tree.

Sign An indication, such as tracks or droppings, of the presence of an animal.

- The Australian brushtail possum (*Trichusorus vulpecula*) was introduced into New Zealand in the late 1800s to establish an export fur trade.
- Only 200–300 possums were released in about 20 locations and now the population is estimated at 70 million.
- Possums spread tuberculosis or TB, which can infect our cattle and deer, resulting in the slaughter of infected stock.
- Possums are nocturnal. Bright sunlight hurts their eyes.
- Possums breed prolifically. As they are a marsupial, females can have a baby on their back, one in the pouch, and be pregnant with another. All the more reason to keep the numbers down!
- Possums have been known to kill and eat young native bird chicks, including our precious kiwi. They love eggs, so will destroy a nest in a matter of seconds.
- Possum skins can earn you up to $10 or more for top-grade skins and plucking the fur can get you about $145 per kilogram – that's about 10 big possums.
- The plucked fur is mixed with merino sheep's wool to make high-quality export goods such as socks, jerseys and hats. It is worth more than $100 million to the economy annually.
- Possum fur is 55 per cent warmer than merino wool and 35 per cent warmer than cashmere (from goats).

A RECIPE TO TRY

POSSUM STEW

INGREDIENTS

1 or 2 possums, meat cut into small cubes
1 tbsp sugar
4 potatoes
1 tsp salt
1 large onion
2 carrots, sliced
6 streaky bacon slices, chopped
thyme and black pepper to taste
2 tbsp olive oil or butter
1 tsp vinegar
1 bay leaf

METHOD

1. Preheat the oven to 160°C. Brown the possum meat in a frying pan. Sprinkle the sugar over the meat as it's browning to caramelise the mixture. Remove and set aside in a bowl.

2. Boil the potatoes in a pot with salted water until they are medium to firm, not soft.

3. Place the onion, carrots, cut-up bacon, thyme and black pepper in the frying pan and cook over a medium heat with the butter or olive oil until just golden in colour.

4. Place the browned meat and carrot-and-onion mixture into a casserole dish, and add a little water mixed with the vinegar. Add the potatoes and bay leaf around the meat in the casserole dish.

5. Place the casserole dish in the oven for 1 hour.

MOUNTAIN SAFETY AND BUSHCRAFT

Whether you are hunting large game, tramping, or hunting with a camera, the moment you set foot into the mountains of New Zealand there are some absolute safety basics that have to be adhered to. Our mountain regions are fabulous places to enjoy, yet they are also death traps for the ill-prepared. Planning is the key. The following suggestions are comprehensive but do not cover every eventuality. Common sense should always be your best guide.

THE WEATHER

The weather can make or break a hunt. It can change in New Zealand seemingly within minutes because of our mountain **terrain** and prevailing wind systems. Rivers can rise in the blink of an eye, claiming lives every year when hunters take a risk and try to cross them. Even with good layers of clothing on, **hypothermia** can set in if the wind chill catches you out in the open. Bad weather can make the track too treacherous to walk, or affect visibility to the extent that you can lose your way without the use of a GPS (global positioning system) device or a compass and map.

What can reasonably be predicted is in the five-day weather forecast. Match this with regular updates before you go into the mountains. If you are ever unsure about whether to chance it, then the saying 'When in doubt, leave it out' should always be your guide.

PRE-TRIP PLANNING

Research the area where you are planning on hunting. Grab hold of topographic maps and learn all about contour lines. Each contour line is a measure of that exact piece of land's height above sea level. When these contour lines move closer and closer together, then the land is becoming steeper. This means that this area will be harder to climb and therefore slower to travel and may in fact be a spot you should avoid altogether.

Another important piece of equipment is a compass. One of the most crucial bits of data it will give you is magnetic north, where the magnetic needle will always point. A compass can be handily attached to the butt or handle of a survival knife. Commonly used in orienteering, the Silva compass is basic and robust in design. With a minimum of practice, you will soon be able to orientate yourself accurately. This means locating your position on the map in relation to where you are on the ground, and then planning your route.

Always stick to the track you are on if it is well marked. If the track has disappeared or you think you are lost, then the compass and a current map will, with a calm head, see you out safely. Beginners should go into the mountains with a more experienced hunter who knows the area well and can demonstrate these skills for you first hand.

Another extremely handy piece of equipment is a GPS device, which can be used in many helpful ways. You can even drop in hut site data or where you hang up a deer to cool, coming directly back to it in the morning. The locations are accurate to within half a metre.

A further safety consideration, especially if you are hunting in remote areas, is to take in a registered PLB (Personal Locator Beacon). Use these only in an emergency, and will guide rescuers right to your location. Mountain radios can be hired from your local sports store or Search and Rescue (SAR) coordinator.

Once you have settled on a hunting area, you must let family or friends know exactly where you are going and what date and time you will be coming out.

And stick to it! Too many people make changes without letting others know, meaning searchers will be looking in the wrong area if you get lost or hurt. It's not worth thinking about, is it?

CLOTHING

The name of the game here is to think layers. Even in summer, a horizontal southerly can blast up the South and North Islands bringing with it below-zero temperatures high up in the ranges. Several loose, thin layers will trap warm air and retain body heat far better than one thick, heavy layer. You can then take a layer off if you need to without warming up too much. Likewise, as the temperature drops, a layer can easily be added.

Comfort is the key, with all gear worn to avoid chafing and restricting movement when wet. A good base layer 'wicks' or draws away body moisture, therefore reducing the risk of this moisture cooling you too quickly. An **insulation** layer is advisable, and then a cover or shell layer.

Even if you are only heading off for a day hunt, you need to plan in case of getting caught out overnight. So include extra insulation top/bottoms and another light coat or poncho. Ponchos are great because they can be rolled up into a coat pocket. This gear must be kept dry — putting it in a large plastic rubbish bag is a good idea. Double-layer the bag to make sure, and stow it near the top of your pack for quick access. A spare warm beanie could mean the difference between life and death, as so much of our body heat exits through our head and neck region.

PACKS AND PACKING

For a day hunt, a day bag and bum bag are fine. There is enough space for that lovely meat you are going to secure, standard emergency clothing and survival items. Blaze orange fabric (as on the pack in the photo) can be seen hundreds of metres away (which doesn't stop you from adding an orange hat and bum bag for good measure). You can also get gear in blaze blue. When carrying a deer, a brightly coloured light jacket should be tied around the animal as an added precaution.

A large pack will fit your overnight gear plus a sleeping bag inside a waterproof cover rolled and tied on the outside. When duck hunting long stretches of river, a pack is invaluable when half a dozen ducks begin to weigh you down when attached to the belt or across the shoulders.

First-aid equipment needs to be easy to get to, particularly in case of an emergency, so placing it in an outside pocket or small compartment is ideal. Take two drink bottles, not one big one — their weight can be more easily distributed around the pack. Many modern packs also have a place to fit a hydration bladder.

Food like scroggin (a mixture of chocolate, nuts and dried fruit) can be included to keep up your blood sugar and energy levels. Poor decisions are most

Tip:
Always test out the weight of your fully laden pack before heading for the mountains.

Tip:
Tie your main coat or poncho over the pack. This ensures you have it on hand when the heavens open up and will also ensure the pack and anything on the outside of it (like a sleeping bag) remains as dry as possible.

commonly made when a hunter becomes tired and/or dehydrated.

Whether your tent or shelter fly should be packed above or below cooking gear is a matter of debate. But if the weather really packs up on you, then a tent may be more important initially than cooking gear, and could even be above spare clothing. Either way, know where you have packed it, because in the dark, cold and wet even the simplest tasks can become extremely difficult.

FOOTWEAR

Footwear that fits well and has suitable tread for the terrain is a must. Day walking shoes are fine on well-maintained tracks and can cover as camp shoes, but they are unsuitable when the weather or uneven surfaces call for waterproofing and a higher supportive cut.

You don't have to spend hundreds of dollars on top-quality boots — but if you do, then look after them. Most new boots come with a container of dubbin. This needs to be rubbed into the leather and especially the stitching so your boots stay waterproof and last as long as possible.

Never dry your boots directly in front of the fire. Simply wash off any mud, ball up newspaper, and stuff this inside the boot to soak up moisture, and place near the fire or outside in a breeze. Leaving them out in the midday sun will harden the leather and make them uncomfortable to wear.

Socks can be too easily taken for granted. Wear two pairs with a thin sports sock under a woollen farm or tramping sock.

Tip:
Most modern boots are designed to be used straight away, but you should always test out your new boots well before that big hunt.

NORTH RIDGE®
FLY TENT
fast FIND
PLB
Freeze Dri
BACK COUNTRY Cuisine
Apple Pie
www.backcountrycuisine.co.nz
ISO-BUTANE
KOVEA
Stormproof Matches
9-hour Candles
Emerge

EQUIPMENT

The following is a list of all that you could need in a basic kit — some of these items are shown in the photo opposite.

- ☐ 2 torches, 1 being a headlamp
- ☐ compass and map
- ☐ GPS
- ☐ knife/Leatherman multi-tool
- ☐ whistle
- ☐ 2 lighters
- ☐ waterproof matches
- ☐ bike tyre tube
- ☐ portable fuel stove
- ☐ toilet paper
- ☐ small travel towel
- ☐ spare laces
- ☐ light 15-metre rope
- ☐ survival blanket
- ☐ poncho
- ☐ waterproof sleeping bag cover
- ☐ paper and pencil
- ☐ extra batteries
- ☐ light extra jacket
- ☐ barley sugars
- ☐ signal mirror
- ☐ folding spade
- ☐ small pruning saw
- ☐ candles
- ☐ water filter or purifying tablets
- ☐ fishing line/hooks
- ☐ toiletries
- ☐ insect repellent
- ☐ several resealable bags
- ☐ several rubbish bags
- ☐ number 8 wire half-loops (can be used for spare tent pegs and billy holders)
- ☐ mobile phone
- ☐ PLB
- ☐ tent fly
- ☐ 5-metre hay-bale binder twine or braided cord
- ☐ scroggin/muesli bars
- ☐ waterproof container of tinder
- ☐ first-aid kit
- ☐ 2 water bottles

When leaving the bush line or crossing over to another track, mark the spot with a small cairn or fern frond pointing to where you have changed direction. Although GPS can do all this for you, of course, it is a simple yet reassuring reminder when heading back to the hut or home.

FITNESS LEVELS

The first priority for safety in our bush and mountain areas is to make sure you are fit before you venture out. Both uphill and downhill slopes can test you if all you have done is walk or jog the flats. Throw a heavy pack on and the effort is doubled.

It is vital that the tramping pace is set by the slowest and/or least experienced person in your party. This will also ensure sound decisions around river crossings and map reading, and ultimately a more comfortable and enjoyable experience. An out-of-breath hunter will not shoot well when an animal is sighted, so take your time.

Out in the bush it is important to take notice of all that is around you, from the sound of rivers to the sun's direction and what the wind is doing, as well as remembering distinctive features like a slip or gnarly old tree. All of these factors will help you keep your sense of direction and can be invaluable when you retrace your steps.

RIVER CROSSING STRATEGIES

Next to falling off a cliff, rivers are the greatest risk areas. Here are some considerations to keep in mind.

1. Do you have to cross? If in doubt, don't.
2. Choose the shallow, wider section, as

the bottom is more likely to be gravel.

3. Aim to angle with the water flow slightly downstream from the entry point.
4. Know where footbridges are from your research and map reading.
5. When by yourself you will need a stout walking stick to lever each time you step, ensuring there are always two points of contact with the river bed.

SHELTER

If you are caught out by the weather, you may need to make a shelter. A lightweight tent fly and binder twine included in your pack can be ultra-quick to set up as a bivouac and may even save your life. An absolute key to shelter building is that you need to be able to get it up quickly if the light or weather is changing fast for the worse, and that you place it in the lee of the wind direction. In other words, site the shelter in a protected spot to lessen the chance of high wind wrecking what you have set up. Don't panic: setting up a good shelter with a fire going will soon get the spirits up. Existing campsites are a good idea, as they are highly likely to be well-selected spots from others using the area. Natural features such as caves or overhangs are ideal if you are caught out, but do check the area, especially the roof, to make sure it won't collapse on you. With a minimum of effort, branches can be dragged and placed on an angle to create a lean-to for added shelter. A lean-

How to tie a bowline knot, one of the most useful knots you will ever learn — perfect for tying a tent fly down.

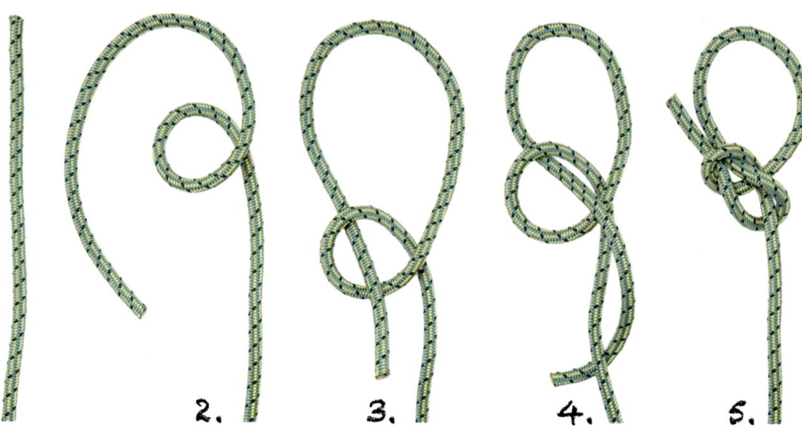

to arrangement can be made by tying your tent fly between two trees at the corners on one edge, and placing logs along the back edge on the ground, creating the right angle for you to get in under the cover. Ensure the back edge is well anchored with anything heavy, and face it towards the oncoming weather. If your tent fly is big enough, then tightly tie a rope between two trees and drape your fly over the rope, making sure both edges reach the ground so that number 8 wire short pegs or logs and rocks can be placed on the edges touching the ground. If no suitable trees can be found, prop up the two ends of the fly with shorter sticks, even 1 metre high is enough. Tie these to the middle of the fly at either end and, just as if you were setting up a tent, brace with rope to pegs or logs, with the central rope running the length of the fly. The stronger the wind, the lower your shelter needs to be. Get the fire going, setting it up carefully so that the warmth radiates back into the shelter but won't burn your tent fly!

BASIC KNOTS

Knowing how to tie basic knots will also serve you well in other areas of life, such as putting up tents on holiday with your family or securing a trailer tarpaulin.

FIRE LIGHTING

Whether you are allowed to light a fire in your chosen area needs to be factored into the trip, as there may be a fire ban in place.

Apart from finding the ideal location for your fire, you should consider the following points:

1. Ignition

Lighters are great, but waterproof matches are just as good.

Tip:
Mix tinder with kindling split from larger firewood or twigs and small dry, dead branches.

Tip:
Short hooks of number 8 wire bent into an 'S' shape are great for holding billies over the fire.

2. Tinder

This is the material used before kindling. You can take in your own tinder in a waterproof container. It can be dry grasses, finely stripped bark or very thin twigs. An old dry bird's nest, pine needles or fine wood-shavings also work well. The length of bike tube you brought in will burn well and hold the flame, as will a carefully placed candle.

3. Kindling

This is a critical phase, as it brings on real flame before firewood is placed on top for warmth or cooking.

4. Firewood

Make sure you have this on hand, as the kindling will soon burn through. Search out a dead dry tree or branch and break it into manageable chunks. Don't waste too much energy on getting the length perfect, as the branch can be fed into the fire as it burns through.

5. Overnighters

Use any big logs, even if they are a little damp, as placing them near the fire will dry them out, and the dampness has the added reward of keeping mozzies away. They will burn slower, too.

FIRST AID AND EMERGENCY

When hunting in our wilderness areas it is important to remember that help can be some distance away. Even the smallest of injuries can become a big problem if you are unprepared.

Minor blisters, stings, cuts, abrasions and strains require no more than common-sense treatment such as a cold soaking in a nearby stream. A decent squirt of antiseptic and appropriate bandaging will deal with most cuts or abrasions.

However, a serious dislocation or sprain around the ankle or knee may require emergency services for a lift out via helicopter. An obvious broken bone needs immediate immobilising to keep it completely still, and, along with serious hypothermia or a bad cut, an air-lift out is the best option. Whatever you do, remain calm. The decisions you make there and then need to weigh up all aspects of the situation.

A FIRST-AID KIT COULD INCLUDE:

- ☐ Band aids
- ☐ Crepe bandage roll
- ☐ Antiseptic spray
- ☐ Triangular bandage
- ☐ Tape
- ☐ Non-adhesive dressings
- ☐ Gauze dressing swabs
- ☐ Splinter forceps
- ☐ Safety pins
- ☐ Notebook and pencil
- ☐ Plastic bags
- ☐ Sunscreen
- ☐ Aspirin
- ☐ Antihistamine
- ☐ Antiseptic cleaning wipes
- ☐ Whistle

LANDSAR [LAND SEARCH AND RESCUE]

The police form the basis of LandSAR, an invaluable organisation which includes experienced members of the Deer Stalkers' Association, members of local tramping clubs, and other volunteers from all walks of life. If you are ever in the position where they are searching for you, remember they will be looking for clues from your route plans that you should have left with friends or family, or notes left in huts.

DID YOU KNOW?

- A GPS device can plot your course, or allow you to mark exactly where you hang a deer in a tree to within a metre or so. It can also show you where you have travelled — but do not leave your compass behind.
- New Zealand is one of the most difficult countries in the world in which to predict the weather. It is not uncommon to experience four seasons in one day in our alpine regions.
- There were 1734 LSAR operations at a cost to the country of $2.9 million in 2012.
- The Southern Alps account for more than double all other rescues undertaken. The weather temperature extremes are far greater and there are more isolated regions away from towns or cities.
- Hunters in the 20 to 29 years age group are the most at risk of hypothermia, and the majority of incidents occur around 3 p.m. in the afternoon when tiredness and low blood-sugar levels kick in. Keep warm and eat regularly!

GLOSSARY

Hypothermia A condition where body temperature drops below normal, and if not treated, can lead to death.

Insulation Layers of clothing to keep body heat in and prevent the cold from getting through.

Terrain The ground or landscape of a particular region.

LARGE ANIMAL HUNTING

Once you understand the importance of mountain safety and bushcraft, you're ready to move on to the business end of serious hunting. In New Zealand this means deer, pigs, goats, tahr and chamois.

BEFORE YOU HUNT

Most of the basic rules for hunting all of these large animals are the same. The hunter must make sure they put into practice all the lessons learned hunting small game. The main difference is that larger animals are even more cunning, and, because you will be searching for them most often in a thick bush or forest environment, you are well and truly in their habitat. They know their exit tracks or escape routes so well that they can disappear so quickly and quietly that you'll wonder whether they were even there in the first place.

SAFETY

In this hunting category you will be using high-powered rifles in challenging surroundings. Visibility might be constantly changing, and your target could be sunning itself on a slope hundreds of metres away, or only a few metres away — close enough

to smell and hear, but not to see.

Blaze orange is a good colour to help you stand out in the bush, and recent research carried out by the New Zealand Police has suggested that blaze blue is the most visible colour in the greatest variety of conditions. All the animals you are hunting are colour-blind, so don't think for one minute that they will spot you any easier than if you were wearing green or brown.

Always carefully identify your target. Before that bolt is closed, before your finger goes on the trigger, you need to be absolutely certain that it is in fact a large animal you are targeting. **If unsure at any stage, then don't fire your gun.** There will be many more deer, but shooting another human will stay with you for the rest of your life.

Splitting up from the hunting party and hunting either too close or not sticking to the agreed areas are prime examples of an incident waiting to happen. The bush helps the hunter get close to their quarry, but it also complicates identification and the backdrop to a shot. It is also far easier to trip over due to the terrain — always make sure your gun is in a safe condition by only loading a round and closing the bolt when you are about to shoot an animal.

When travelling in a group, only the front person should have their gun loaded but also safe, with the **bolt** semi-open and **safety** on. If you're behind your mate, always be aware of where that barrel is pointing.

GUNS

You need a serious bullet calibre here to achieve the clean, one-shot kill all hunters are after out of respect for the animal and the sport. Deciding on the calibre to use depends on a number of factors:

1. How large and strong-willed will your quarry be?
2. At what distances are you likely to be firing a round?

3. Your age and size with regard to your ability to absorb the recoil.

Early deer cullers were highly proficient with .222 calibre; especially the meat hunters, as the lighter bullet made for minimum damage and the quieter shot wouldn't disturb other deer in the area. There are two important factors to consider, though. First, they were hunting continually and shooting deer in numbers we can only dream about. So they were likely to be crack shots with all that live practice. Second, they also knew exactly where to place the bullet for a quick kill in all situations. Generally, the lighter the bullet, the lighter the recoil and **muzzle blast**, but also the less 'killing power' on larger animals.

Flinching as a result of high recoil and muzzle blast can seriously affect your accuracy and lead to habits that are hard to break. It just isn't pleasant knowing that firing a shot will bring discomfort, especially when you're lying down, as you can't absorb the recoil as easily as when standing. Recoil can be reduced, along with muzzle blast, by using a **suppressor** attached to the barrel. This is well worth exploring with your local gun store.

The best place to aim at is the traditional kill zone behind the shoulder area, at the heart and lungs. Any shot hitting an animal directly in a vital area at close or moderate distances will take it out regardless of the calibre. But knowing your gun's limitations and perhaps your own shooting ability at greater distances should encourage you to learn the art of stalking. Get in close and place that shot carefully! As a beginning hunter, if you are young and slight of build, then something around the .223 or .243 calibre are excellent choices. The added bonus, apart from the cheaper cost of a firearm and ammunition with lighter calibre, is that it can be used on long-range **varminting** or rabbit or hare shots. Goats or wallabies are also perfect options with these lighter calibres.

This doesn't mean that armed with a large-calibre 130 to 180 grain

large calibre

small calibre

bullet, as with a .270 or .300 Winchester magnum, you will dispatch a deer with a shot just anywhere around the chest either. There are specific regions you should be aiming for, and the angle of the bullet pathway into an animal above or below you needs to be carefully considered. Sometimes shots at deer slightly back-on or facing towards you on an angle require the hunter to imagine the pathway of the bullet, making necessary adjustments to ensure you target the heart or lungs.

WHERE TO HUNT

Nothing beats listening in to conversations about local hunting areas. It can provide highly valuable information about access across farmland.

DOC or the regional council pest team will also provide sound advice on areas with good numbers to safely hunt. It is advisable to get a hunting permit for national park

Tip:
As a safety measure, just remember to always expect other hunters in your area.

land but be aware that, while DOC doesn't formally monitor hunting pressure, they do have a reasonable idea on a local level of just how much is going on. On the flip side, you can pick their brains over likely hotspots. Your local hunting or fishing store will also point you in the right direction.

HOW TO HUNT

Once you reach an area where there are signs of animal life, all your senses have to be on high alert. Slow down and stop frequently. Try to notice everything to get what is called a 'feel for the bush'. Notice unusual landforms, bent trees on ridges and open slips. Store it all away to remember next time. It also helps in keeping your sense of direction. Using a small camera or your phone is a great way to build up a visual record of a hunting area.

As with rabbit and hare hunting, the wind direction is most critical of all. The hunt has to be planned around the direction of the wind. All large animals have a keen sense of smell — none more so than pigs, which makes up for their poor eyesight. There will be times when you can smell the quarry, but still can't compete with them or a well-trained dog. A dog trained to stay at your side to 'wind' animals can be deadly — it will indicate an animal's presence well before you both stumble upon them.

The route you take, while always considering the wind, will inevitably lead you along walking trails left by the animals of the forest, from possums to large game. Other signs you are looking for are droppings, which if fresh (less than a day old) will still be shiny. The older the droppings, the drier they get. Prints sometimes off to the side of the track or just down from a small slip are dead giveaways. Use all your senses, but slow your pace right down when the sign is prevalent. Stop frequently, taking in everything around you, and listen intently as the wind will carry sounds toward you.

whitetail deer droppings

Often 'tail-end Charlie' (the last person in a line) can spot an animal down a gully a stone's throw away, popping its head up just as the front hunters move past it. Various places seem to just cry out 'action'. This is where you should sit down for a while, **glassing** into shadowy spots with your binoculars. You might even catch the faintest of movements, like the flick of an ear in the shadows, as long as you stay absolutely still.

Always try to stalk extremely slowly once you know an animal is nearby. Regularly stopping — or 'still hunting', as it is called — gives the advantage to the hunter. When a good **field of view** presents itself, stop immediately, and use a tree trunk or bush to further break up your outline.

When an animal is spotted, you need to use every piece of cover between you and it as you move closer. Take just a few steps or crawl, as a nervy hind (female deer) will vary the amount of time it spends eating and will catch you out if you try to cover too much ground between you and it. Don't keep staring at the animal for too long, as they seem to have a **sixth sense** and get fidgety and move away. Don't expect to see the whole animal in the cover. Train your eye to pick out an ear twitching or parts of the animal's shape — but always remember you must identify your target accurately before firing.

Always have your rifle in both hands at

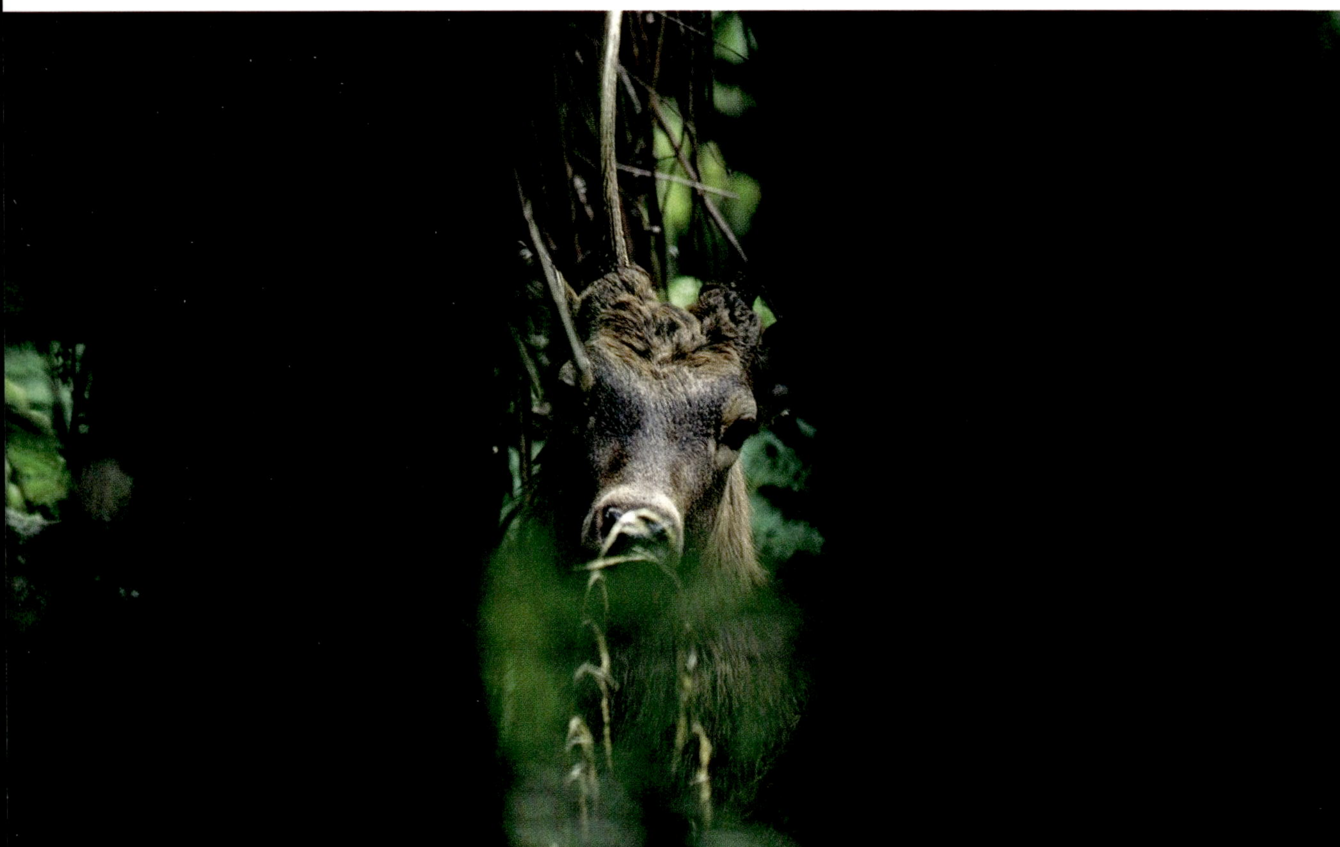

Tip:
Only move when the animal dips its head to eat or forage.

belt level and move ever so slowly, bringing it to your shoulder when you decide the time is right for a shot. You will only have a couple of precious seconds to line up and fire, but fast movements will mean you might miss your opportunity, and see a 'disappearing rump' more often than not. Red deer seem to allow very little time for a shot, but more curious species may stay that little bit longer. This makes it even more important to practise shooting from different positions. You often won't have time to get perfectly comfortable. If you're standing, simply lean in towards a branch. This will provide excellent support before you fire.

A fit hunter will always make better choices in the mountains both safety-wise and with their shooting performance. So get fit before you start hunting large animals. It is their domain. An unfit hunter moving too fast and then trying to hold a rifle steady has far less chance of getting a solid shot into an animal, killing it humanely. Likewise, unfit people are liabilities for others in their hunting party and for those called out to find them because they have taken on more than they can handle or get lost due to poor decision-making when tired.

WHEN TO HUNT

All large game animals prefer warm places. North-facing slopes are likely spots to find animals feeding or resting up, chewing their cud, from mid-morning to mid-afternoon. They will be lapping up the sun from late autumn through to spring. So be on the lookout for those open spots, but whatever you do, do not march straight into or onto them. Try to approach them from above, and if possible use binoculars to search out these spots from vantage points. In summer, animals will often be found resting up just inside the bush edge in the shade. A good set of binoculars is indispensable, as they gather in available light and can reveal resting animals. The absolute best times to hunt are early morning and late afternoon to early evening before the light goes.

DEER HUNTING

THE ROAR

The roar is the time of year from late March to May when stags will be roaring to scare off other stags and to gather in hinds to mate with. The roar is an excellent time to deer hunt, especially for stags, as they lose caution and will roar to warn other stags away from their hinds, letting you in on their locality. Sometimes they will challenge your own roar and come right up to your spot, making for an easier shot.

You can imitate a stag's roar by blowing into a hollowed-out bull horn or tube. This can entice a stag, sounding just like a wily old competitor. (But be wary, this has led to hunters becoming the hunted!) Sometimes the lowest of grunty rumbles is all that is required to get a response from a dense pocket of bush, so don't think you have to blow with everything you have — risking an inaccurate sound will send the stag hightailing it away from your spot. There are commercial calls that will cover most deer roars, and some multi-purpose callers even include feral goat calls.

A condition known as 'buck fever', a nervous excitement at the first hint of game, can sometimes affect hunters — all the more reason to stick to the ground rules. It is also far safer to keep away from highly popular areas during the roar. The roar is the time when most incidents seem to happen in the bush. Hats, bush shirts, slip-on vests, long pants, bum bags and even packs come in blaze orange or blue, so wear as much of it as you can. The added advantage of light vests is that they can be tied to an animal you may be carrying out of the bush — if looking through thick scrub, a deer on a hunter's back can be mistaken for a live animal, especially if the head is still attached.

bull horn

WHERE TO HUNT DEER

In New Zealand we have numerous species of deer to choose from.

Red deer are the most common and spread from Stewart Island right up to the Far North. They can be found at the highest altitudes in the South Island right down to small scrubby farm blocks at sea level. But this doesn't necessarily make them an easy target. If they get the drop on you, they will exit rapidly, barely making a sound, sometimes making you wonder whether or not you just saw a large bird!

Fallow deer can occupy even the thinnest strip of scrubby gully cover on farmland, sometimes well away from the main forest. They can be found throughout New Zealand, except in Northland and Taranaki. They are an easier deer to hunt as they stay longer to check out an intruder in their territory. They are also a smaller deer and therefore lighter to carry out. Their skins are easy to **tan**, and make for super rugs.

Sambar are found in only a few spots of the middle North Island from Horowhenua to Whanganui, in coastal swamps and scrub. They are the most nocturnal of our deer species, making them hard to locate and shoot. A heavy species, they require larger calibres to bring down cleanly. Whitetail, sika and rusa are very similar, in that they have a small territory but it will be in, or have access to, heavy cover.

Whitetails can be found only on Stewart Island and in the Lake Wakatipu region. Their habitats can be so dense the hunter has to crawl under scrub. Often hunters have more success finding a clear area and sitting still or in a tree waiting for them to move along one of the game trails. Whitetails can sometimes also be caught on the beach nibbling seaweed.

Sika are a beautiful deer found in the Kaweka and Kaimanawa ranges of the North Island. They are rarely found out in the open. Hunting the edges of clearings is more profitable. The stag roar sounds like a donkey.

Rusa are found mainly in the Kaimanawas and are considered to be the fastest runners, letting out a loud honk as they depart, with habits very similar to the sika.

Wapiti deer are mainly found in Fiordland and are very difficult to find, even though they can grow to up to 450 kilograms!

Chamois and **tahr** are both large goat-like animals, usually found far higher

Whitetail

Sika

Chamois

Tahr

up than deer, and only in the South Island. Tahr are native to Nepal and India, but were introduced to New Zealand in the early days to the Southern Alps, mountains that provide a similar habitat to their home in the central Himalayas. Chamois were introduced to New Zealand in 1907 from the Austrian Alps, and are considered a prized **trophy**, but one of the most difficult to secure.

Tahr tend to cling to the upper bush line and scree slopes. Chamois are the more adventurous and can be found at sea level on the West Coast right up to the mountaintops.

The best time to hunt both is early and late in the day when they are easier to spot because they are on the move feeding. It can be frustrating trying to spot both species when they are lying down, as their coats — especially their summer ones — blend in with their rocky surroundings.

On public land the pressure of helicopter shooting and other hunters on foot may have changed chamois and tahr behaviour, and you might find more in low scrubby regions away from high-pressure disturbance areas. Trophies can still be gathered in public regions and, apart from the horns, the winter coats on both animals can look stunning when properly tanned and spread on the floor.

PIG HUNTING

If this is a form of hunting that really grabs you, then seek out a pig-hunting club or an experienced person, and soak up that vital information. This is an area requiring clear thinking and keen knowledge of the hunting grounds, as even highly proficient pig hunters can have very serious accidents. Pigs can be hunted successfully without the use of dogs, but, as pigs frequent thicker undergrowth for large parts of the day, they can be hard to find without them. Pig dogs need to be well trained or you could be biting off more than you can chew – wild pigs are capable of doing some real damage to either the dogs or yourself. You also need to be fit and strong to carry these animals out of the bush.

wild goats

GOAT HUNTING

Feral goats can be found just about anywhere in New Zealand. They really are a pest, trying out any plant to decide whether they like it or not, and can decimate a forest floor. They can be found in big numbers, and the trick is to get above and downwind from them. If you do, you can usually fire multiple shots, securing a number of animals at a time. Goat skins, especially black-and-white combinations, can make for attractive rugs, while the horns can be trophies in themselves. Dogs can also be highly effective on goats. Their sense of smell will of course indicate to the dog just where the animals are, and in some cases, if particularly well trained, they can be let off their lead to round up the goats, bringing them towards you. Make sure you place yourself above the goats so you can take close shots, but take real care as a high-powered round can easily go through a goat and endanger the dog if it's directly behind the mob.

SKINNING AND BUTCHERING LARGE GAME

The methods used on large game are much the same as with skinning and cutting up rabbits. It is a lot easier to tie up the back legs of the animal, running the rope over a branch and hoisting it up before starting. When pulling out the intestine, it is important you do two things:

1. Cut around the anus to ensure this detaches along with the intestines.
2. Cut away the larynx or throat that detaches from the top of the chest

Tip:
A good dog will track wounded animals over great distances.

cavity. Meat can go off very quickly in hot or warm weather, and this allows air to circulate, aids in cooling the meat, and lessens the chance of flies laying eggs where you can't see them.

1. An example of a large fold-away pocket knife with a good blade for gutting and even skinning large game. 2. A skinning specialist. 3. A curved blade with a wooden handle, a standard New Zealand butcher variety that many hunters will keep on their belt. 4. A knife designed for pig-sticking.

Cleaning out the chest cavity with long grass and covering the carcass in mutton cloth or game bags will keep the flies away. Do not place the meat in plastic bags until you are ready to freeze it. Freshly killed meat in plastic bags sweats and goes off super-quick. In hot weather, get someone to show you how to butcher the animal fairly promptly or take it to a local butcher. Many an animal can be wasted by leaving it hanging in the barn for too long.

- A high-powered rifle can send a bullet over 4.5 kilometres.
- Male deer or stags grow antlers each year and fight others stags with them. These antlers make excellent home-made knife handles.
- Most deer species are born with white spots on their coat. It is thought this is to help with their motionless camouflage when lying in vegetation.
- Deer can live up to 20 years of age.
- Whitetails will seek out seaweed to nibble on right at the shore edge.
- Wild pigs use their snouts to dig up tasty grubs and roots. This action is called 'pig rooting' and can wreck a farmer's pasture if pig numbers are high.
- Goats were domesticated as far back as 7000 BC, and a group of goats is known as a 'trip'.
- Tahr have a rubber-like core in their hooves which is incredibly flexible.
- Chamois are related to the antelope family, and their hide (in the form of a 'chammy') can be used to wipe down cars after they have been washed.
- .50 calibre air rifles firing at 4000 psi (pounds per square inch) and over 1000 feet per second are powerful enough to kill deer.

GLOSSARY

Blaze orange Also called **safety orange**. The colour used most often for high-visibility clothing because it contrasts in particular with the blue of the sky and sets anyone wearing it apart from their surroundings.

Bolt The part of a firearm that blocks the rear of the chamber while the propellant burns, but moves out of the way to allow another cartridge or shell to be inserted in the chamber.

Field of view The area that is visible.

Glassing Using binoculars to search out animals.

Muzzle blast The rapid expulsion of hot, high-pressure gases when the gun is fired.

Safety Also called the **safety catch**. A mechanism that helps prevent the accidental discharge of a firearm in order to ensure safer handling.

Sixth sense Knowing there is danger without an animal's five senses of sight, hearing, touch, smell and taste being necessarily involved.

Suppressor The attachment screwed onto the end of the barrel designed to reduce recoil and muzzle blast.

Tan To cure the animal skin.

Trophy An item made from part of the body of an animal (often its head mounted on a plaque) that serves as a reminder of the success of hunting it.

Varminting Hunting small animals that are troublesome pests.

GOAT STEW

INGREDIENTS

4 kg small chunks of meat (better from the back legs and back straps), cut into 1.5 cm cubes
2 tsp salt
3 large onions, sliced and broken up
¼ cup olive oil or vegetable oil
¾ cup flour
8 cups beef stock
3 large tomatoes, peeled and sliced
1 green pepper, sliced
10 garlic cloves, pressed
2 tsp oregano
1½ tsp ground pepper

METHOD

1. Put a large pan on the stove element at medium high.

2. Add the meat, salt and chopped onions and brown for a few minutes in the oil.

3. Stir in the flour and brown lightly.

4. Add the remaining ingredients. Mix well, turn down the heat to low and simmer covered until tender.

TARGET SHOOTING AND ARCHERY

If you want to improve your ability to shoot accurately, then target shooting is a great way to do it. Even if you are just looking for a bit of fun, you do not need any gear, just turn up to a club and it is all there ready for you.

You will soon find there is no end to the different kinds of targets available to you. These include metal targets that drop down when the pellet hits them, making a loud sound on contact, or numbered targets that allow for accurate scoring, much the same as indoor competitive shooting.

Everyone is encouraged to join small-bore indoor target shooting groups, usually from age 10, but if you are under 18 a parent or caregiver will be expected to come with you if you are using an air gun and you must be supervised by a licence holder if you are using a firearm. It is best to contact the club before turning up so that an experienced shooter can help you.

THE THREE MAIN TYPES OF TARGET SHOOTING

1. Small **bore** (.22 calibre, usually at 25 metres indoors and at 50 metres outdoors).

2. Big bore (.308 calibre, usually over distances from 300 to 900 metres).
3. Air rifles (over 10 metres).

Tip:
The range fee should cover a club rifle, gear hire (including elbow pads and a gun rest if needed), spotting scope, ammunition and coaching.

The bullets provided will all be soli which greatly improves accuracy.

The average cost for a target shooting session is around $10 for 12 shots at 10 different targets. The eleventh (or middle) target is used to warm up and practise a few shots to ensure the gun is shooting accurately. These targets will be clearly marked so you can tell them apart from the others.

Often one of the spotters (the person who will check how you are shooting with spotting scopes) will tell you to adjust the top or side peep sight (see page 93) dials a certain amount of 'clicks'. If you are new, someone will help you to do this before your next shot.

Your score is based on how close your bullet hole is to the centre of the target. The strike is determined by the outer edge of the bullet hole. The target is subdivided into decimal score zones, with a bullseye, a central ring, and nine successive rings which are each separate score zones. Remember, the smaller the zone the higher the points! You will receive a score of 10 if you hit the bullseye, and a score of 1 if you hit the outer ring of the target. If you strike a line between rings you will be given the lower score of the two. Each ring of the target is broken down further into 10 decimal score zones. If your bullet hits the inner bullseye without touching the first ring around it, you will get a shot score of 10.1, a perfect score! If your bullet hits the bullseye but part of the hole it makes is touching the first ring, your score will be 10. The highest score you can achieve over the 10 targets is 100.10 (10 times 10.1). Likewise, if you shot all 9s, then a score of 90 would be achieved. A decimal or inner bullseye on one of the targets when combined with 9 other scores of 9 would give the shooter a score of 90.1.

If you are a beginner, you can start your shooting practice using a gun rest until you are more comfortable with the weight of the gun.

SIGHTS

All three forms of shooting rely on the same sighting system, called 'peep sights' or 'peeps'. No other sights are allowed. The sighting system consists of two very small holes built into adjustable sights on the barrel of the gun. The main adjustable peep sight is close to the shooter's eye. This is lined up with the other peep sight, attached to the far end of the barrel, as you place the black spot of the target directly in the middle of both peeps.

BREATHING

You need to be very calm and patient when shooting. Feeling relaxed will lower your pulse rate and improve your breathing before squeezing the trigger. The lower you can get your heart rate, the stiller you will hold the rifle, making your shot much more accurate. If you are too impatient you are likely to miss the target altogether! Here is a simple approach that will improve your scores with practice and consistent preparation.

1. Get into a comfortable body position. Lie on the ground and spread your legs. If you are a right-handed shooter, bring your right leg up slightly and bend it to provide a steadier base for your body.

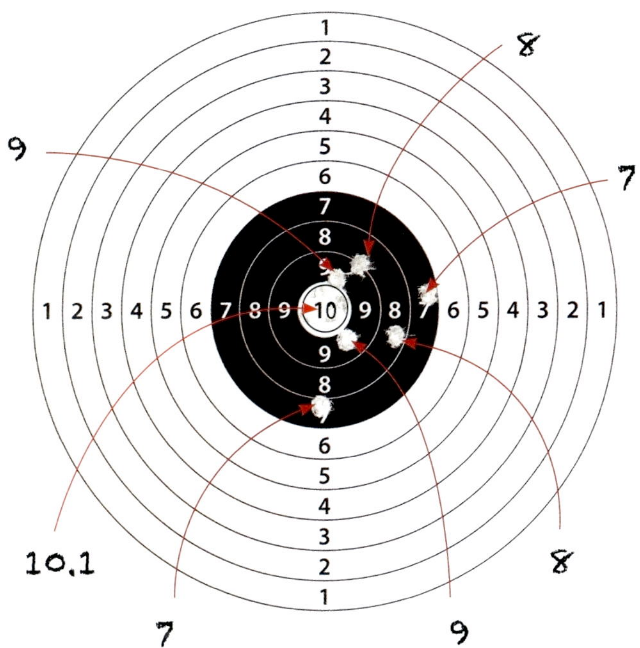

2. All shoots start with the very middle or 'sighter' targets. You will have two or three sighters, which will not be counted in your score, so you can warm up and ensure your sights are correct. It is important that you move ever so slightly when adjusting to each target. After two or three sighters, the range officer should be able to give corrections to your sight if needed.
3. Count two-and-a-half breaths. Then as you take a half breath in, the target should naturally align with the centre of your peep sights. This is when you need to squeeze the trigger.

Tip:
Get to know the trigger pressure on your gun. The triggers on target rifles are very light and sensitive, which means they will react quickly when you squeeze – knowing exactly when a round is going off is crucial to accuracy, so get to know the trigger pressure.

RANGE SAFETY RULES

1. All ranges have a safety officer who must be obeyed at all times.
2. All guns must be handled with care. The **breech** must be open and unloaded when the gun is being carried.
3. Do not touch any gear other than your own.
4. Only load your gun when the safety officer allows the group to commence.
5. Remain on the mound until you are told you can leave.
6. When told to 'cease fire' all guns are to be unloaded, breeches opened and placed beside you.
7. No alcohol or drugs are allowed on the range.

ARCHERY

There are different types of archery which include different distances and disciplines. They are all great fun! A bonus is that you can practise your archery skills safely in your own backyard, with targets and a secure backdrop which will catch any stray arrows. If you practise from a young age, you could successfully hunt big game animals, like deer, with a compound bow later on in life.

comfortable shooting position

FIELD ARCHERY

The natural setting of field archery is very popular with beginners and 'old hands' alike, with trees, scrub, high grasses and tracks to walk from target to target. The scenery is different at each shoot-off place, and distances vary to each target from 5 metres out to 50 metres. A circuit, or loop, of all the targets usually lasts about one-and-a-half to two hours. Targets can sometimes take on different animal shapes, and you may even see some in 3D!

TARGET ARCHERY

The two types of bow used for target archery are the recurve bow and the compound bow. The recurve bow is traditional and the one used by Katniss in the movie *The Hunger Games*. Recurve archery is the only discipline of archery included at the Olympic Games. The compound bow is modern, made using layers of laminated wood and has a pulley system. There are clubs all around New Zealand which will usually provide a minimum of three half-hour sessions and a two-hour 'fit to shoot' programme. Both types of target archery can involve competitions from 30 to 90 metres.

Tip:
Never be tempted to draw your bow and release the string without releasing or firing an arrow. The arrow absorbs most of the energy of the string when fired, and 'dry firing' means the energy is absorbed by the bow instead. This increases the chances of damaging or even breaking the bow.

target arrow head

hunting arrow head

BOW HUNTING

This form of hunting is becoming more and more popular. Seasoned rifle enthusiasts, who have hunted large animals like deer or pigs for years, are switching to the silent bow. The challenge is a very simple one: get as close as you can. The maximum distance to consistently pull off killing shots is well within 80 metres and probably more like 40 to 50 metres. Being able to stalk using every one of your senses, and being extremely patient waiting for that side-on or facing shot requires a high level of fitness, self-awareness and confidence with your equipment. Experienced rifle hunters say it is like being new to the sport again and revisiting very early lessons — but that is what makes it all the more enjoyable! Diehard deer stalkers will claim that a hunt on goats with a bow can bring just as much satisfaction. In fact, goats are an excellent choice of large animal to stalk, and, for those new to hunting, a way to find out how good their bow and arrow skills are in the field.

Hunting arrows are sharp enough to shave the hairs off your arm. Please don't try it at home! The arrow heads have edges designed to slice into the toughest of animal hides and on through vital organs and **arteries** to ensure a quick death. When combined with a powerful compound bow, an arrow can pass right through a large animal and travel further on into the bush. It is important, then, that basic firearm safety rules and guidelines are followed at all times.

The bow hunter can build a set-up in the backyard, making practice far more convenient. It is not against the law to practise with your bow in a built-up area, but common-sense safety procedures should always be your guide. Backdrop safety is vital — make sure no one will wander across your practice area unaware of what you are doing.

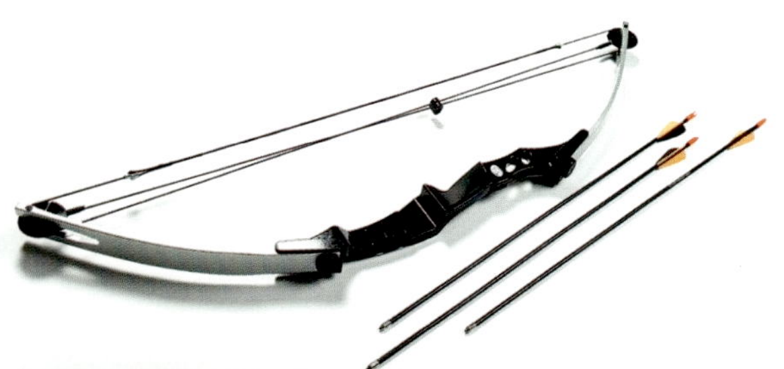

BOW FISHING

Koi carp is the main quarry of bow fishing due to their size and habit of feeding near the surface of the water. Unlike trout, which are protected, they are considered a pest in our waterways so there is no ethical problem in shooting as many as you can. They are not all that nice to eat, but the family cat or neighbour's cat will gladly polish them off. A reel can be attached to the bow with nylon to retrieve your fish and arrow.

A golden koi carp, targeted by bow hunters in the Waikato lakes and the Waikato River.

DID YOU KNOW?

- Way back in 2800 BC, Egyptians were using the first compound bow held together with animal sinew (the tough bone connecting material such as ligaments and tendons) and glue.
- An arrow could pierce body armour in the early days of warfare.
- The bow is still used in intertribal warfare in Central Africa and South America. There have also been bow-related deaths in Papua New Guinea.
- Legend has it that William Tell was forced to shoot an apple off his son's head using a crossbow.
- A Japanese archer has shot an arrow 70 metres right down the end of a previous arrow, completely splitting the first arrow perfectly. Check it out on YouTube.
- Target shooting is an Olympic sport and is taken very seriously by a great number of countries around the world.

GLOSSARY

Arteries Blood vessels that take blood away from the heart.

Bore The inside of a gun's barrel.

Breech Where the bullet or shot shell is placed ready for firing.

BAIT FISHING IN SALT AND FRESH WATER

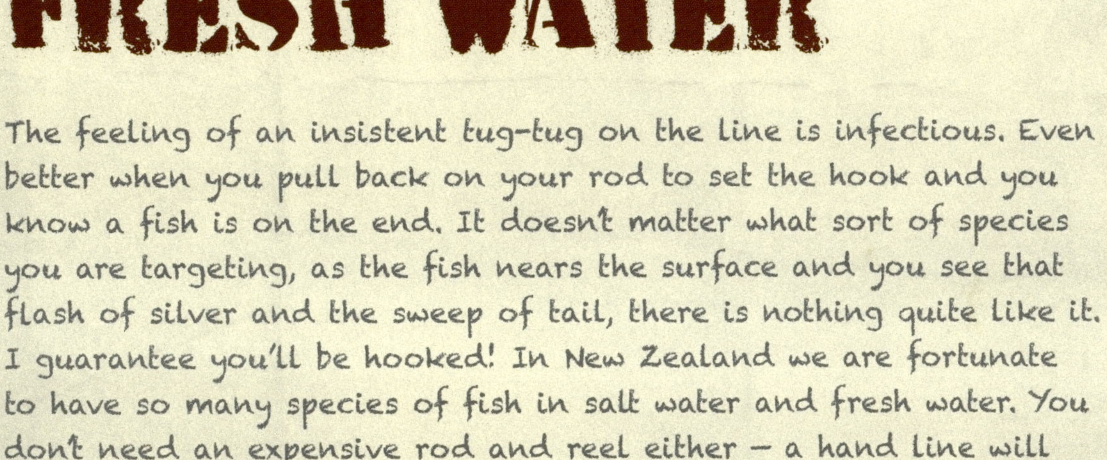

The feeling of an insistent tug-tug on the line is infectious. Even better when you pull back on your rod to set the hook and you know a fish is on the end. It doesn't matter what sort of species you are targeting, as the fish nears the surface and you see that flash of silver and the sweep of tail, there is nothing quite like it. I guarantee you'll be hooked! In New Zealand we are fortunate to have so many species of fish in salt water and fresh water. You don't need an expensive rod and reel either – a hand line will do in most situations.

HOW TO FISH

HAND LINES

Hand lines are cheap and easy to carry. They can be made from any length of cord, cotton string or nylon wrapped around a stick, spool or, perhaps best of all, an old soft-drink bottle. To make a hand line, simply wind the line around the stick, spool or bottle. Attach a sinker to the end of the line and tie on a baited hook further up the line with a **trace**. Lower the line into the water until the sinker hits the bottom, then hold the line with your thumb and forefinger, making sure the line is tight. You can tell that a fish is biting when you feel a tug or a nibble. When you do, quickly yank the line backward so the hook lodges into the fish's mouth, before steadily pulling up the line, making sure it doesn't go loose, or the fish might be able to flick the hook out and get away!

A soft-drink bottle works really well as a hand line. Make a small hole in the neck of the bottle and thread one end of the nylon through. Wind 20–30 metres of nylon around the thinnest part of the bottle. Hold the bottle by the neck with one hand, while holding onto the line with the other, just above the hooks. Now start swinging the short length of line in a clockwise direction two or three times and let go as the sinker swings towards the water and area you want it to land.

Hand lines can be made at home or bought in a local fishing store, ready to go.

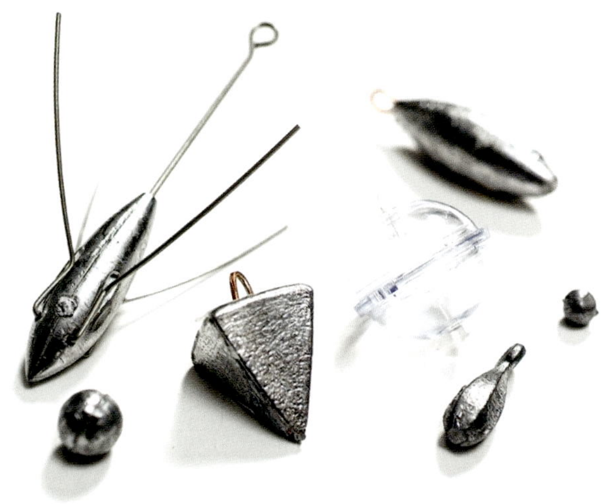

Your selection of sinker needs to match the nylon strength of your line. You'll need a heavier sinker with strong nylon if there is strong wave action or currents. This will help to keep the line in one place. The sand grabber sinker with the wire sticking out is great for sandy beaches.

Use a 'fisherman's knot' to tie sinkers, lures and hooks onto fishing lines.

1. First pass the line through the eye of the sinker, lure or hook, double back and make five or six turns around the line.
2. Hold the coils in place with your finger and thread the end of the line through the first loop just above the eye, then back through the large loop.
3. Pull the knot tight with both hands.

Get an experienced fisherman to show you the other important knots you should learn before going out fishing. These include a loop knot, to tie the sinker onto the end of your line, a blood knot, for joining two lines together, and a trace knot, for joining a trace to the main line.

HOOKS

Generally, hooks in the beak shape or octopus-style in anything from size 4/0 right through to 10/0 can be used for most fish. For small target fish such as herrings and spotties, you could even use smaller fly-fishing hooks.

Two baited hooks will increase the smell of bait in the water, and, at slightly different depths, can attract different fish species. The lower hook will often catch spotties and cod, whereas herrings will take the top hook. When fishing for perch, trout or eels, just the one hook is enough, particularly with eels, as they can tangle a line quicker than you can say ‘I’ve got one!’ If the fish are feeding near the surface, then a float with a 30-centimetre trace hanging down can be deadly, especially with herrings or cruising kahawai.

Be very careful baiting a hook and never rush. Hooks can easily attach to your fingers, and when they do it can be very painful! Pinch the bait between your thumb and forefinger. Hold the hook in the other hand and bring the hook gently through the bait, making sure the point of the hook shows through the bait. A wriggly worm needs to be threaded through a couple of times to stay on the hook!

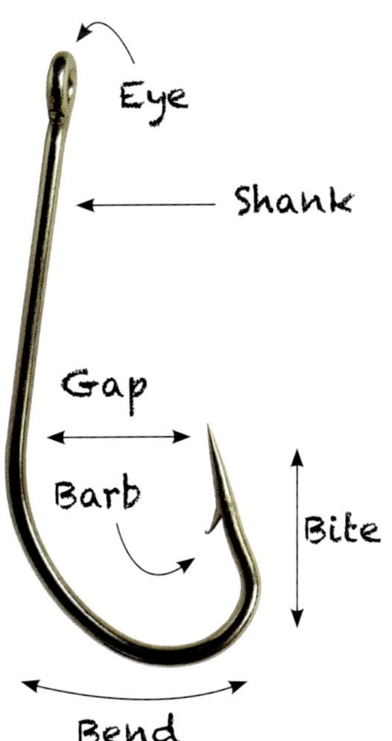

Tip:

Before you start fishing, stretch the nylon line on a fence before winding it onto the reel – this will greatly reduce tangles. Simply tie the end to a fence post and walk the nylon reel along the fence, pulling it tight and looping it around a post 3 or 4 metres away, then back again. Keep going to and fro until the nylon is completely off the spool. Make sure the nylon is stretched tightly. Leave for a day or more, then tie one end onto your spinning reel and start winding the line back onto the reel. Take your time and make sure even the smallest of tangles doesn't get left on the reel or it will drastically affect the casting of the line.

SPINNING RODS

Spinning rods give you more control of the fishing line. They are designed to hold a spinning reel just above the bottom handle. The reel holds your fishing line and helps you feed out and retrieve the line much faster. The rod helps you to **cast** the line further. A regular 2 to 2.5 metre spinning or casting rod is capable of catching just about any fish out there, so it is a good all-rounder in fresh and salt water.

Whether you should buy a two-, three- or four-piece rod depends on how you will be transporting it. Each one can cast and catch just as effectively as the other, but a

Kahawai

four-piece rod in a tube can be tucked away in a pack if you have to walk a long way to your fishing spot. However, the standard two-piece rod is cheaper and easy to put together because it only has one join.

Fibreglass rods are a good choice for beginners because they are extremely strong, but as you improve your spinning skills and develop as a fisherperson a graphite rod will add length, control and feel to casting and catching fish. Another option is a telescopic rod. As the name suggests, these rods are made up of pieces that slot into each other and collapse down to make them easier to carry. They are especially popular with back-country fishers.

As with anything new, you need to practise to cast that bait right where you want it. So tie a round sinker onto your fishing line using a fisherman's knot (no hook just yet), and practise casting to targets on the back lawn or at a park — always checking of course that no one will wander into your practice area. (See the 'Practising your cast' section on page 117 for further tips on how to cast.)

A standard spinning reel will serve you well in most situations. A four-piece rod like this can even be stowed into a pack for a spot of fishing high up in the mountains!

mullet

SURFCASTING

The equipment used for surfcasting is larger and a bit more expensive than spinning equipment. Surfcasting rods are anything from 3 to nearly 5 metres in length, and the reels are usually much larger because they need to accommodate stronger nylon, which is of course much thicker. You must also put in a bit more time cleaning your rod and reel after use, as the salt can cause corrosion or affect the moving parts.

The aim with a surfcasting rod is to cast out past the waves. The back of the last wave is an excellent spot as the sand won't have been stirred up there. Practice with casting will soon let you know what the better sinker weight is — usually a 4- to 6-ounce works well. A sinker that is too heavy for the nylon may snap it when casting or place too much strain on the rod tip, causing it to break. If the area you are fishing has strong currents, then sinkers with wire sticking out (called 'sand grabbers') are worth using to keep the line in place.

Reels are best if they are the spinning or fixed-spool type. They should also have nylon with a breaking strain of 5 to 10 kilograms and at least 200 metres of length. Besides the fact that it is always safer to fish with someone else, one of you could cast as far as you can and the other just far enough to clear the first few waves. You might end up catching cruising kahawai at maximum casting distance or mullet chasing small herrings closer to the shore. Both kahawai and mullet are delicious to eat, as long as they are bled as soon as they are landed by cutting across below the gills.

Don't leave any fish you have caught out in the sun, as fish can go off and spoil very quickly. Gut them and keep them as cool as possible in a damp sack in the shade, or in a chilly bin. The guts can be frozen and used later as **burley**.

BAIT

What bait you use should match what your target fish is eating, so do your research. Shop-bought bait like squid or bonito will often be effective, while using herrings that you have caught can be perfect if you're fishing for kahawai and blue or red cod. Your local fishing store can provide you with tips for specific fish and the bait that works best.

To attract more fish to your spot, you could use a burley sack. This can be made out of an onion sack stuffed with crushed-up shellfish, fish guts and fish heads — just about anything that is edible. Pierce holes in it, lower it into the water on a length of cord if you're wharf or boat fishing, and watch the fish come in. Crayfish-bait pots on a thin cord, which are small and easily carried in a day pack, or **pikau** made from a sack, can be placed either side of the fishing lines.

Little chunks of paua are great in situations where lots of small fish try to nibble the bait off before your target species gets a chance, as their tough texture helps them stay on the hook. Not a lot can beat crushed-up cat's-eye sea snails around the rocks as the tide comes in — go on and try it. Crush the snail with a handy stone and pierce the firm part of the snail meat with the hook. Make sure the hook's point is just poking through.

squid

WHERE TO FISH

SALT WATER

Land-based saltwater fishing could find you fishing off a wharf, standing on rocks, or casting from the beach. Always be aware of what the waves are doing and never fish by yourself, even if you are a good swimmer. Always check the weather forecast — and

when in doubt, don't risk it.

If you're fishing off the beach or surfcasting, study the stretch of water carefully and look for the calmer water near rips or at the back of the very last wave — fish will be using the current as they feed. They prefer not to come into stirred-up, sandy water because it gets in their gills and affects their visibility as they hunt.

Your local fishing store will guide you to the top spots to fish and the most effective bait to use. Don't be afraid to talk to others who are fishing at the same spot as you, and keep an eye on their techniques to pick up some valuable pointers. Sometimes the fish are feeding in different ways and it can be very hard to catch anything, but there will be days when the fish hit the line before it makes it to the bottom and the action is fast and furious.

The best time to fish is when the tide is on the turn, which means it has reached low tide and has started to come in. This is when the action can really heat up, especially with rock fishing, as the fish

Tip:
Kahawai feed on herrings and small mackerel, so one method that works well is to use silver kahawai spinners. A kahawai caught on light trout rod tackle is real sport as they can often put up a fight.

start to move over the rocky bed closer to shore to feed. Blue cod in particular love the rocky bottom. They are also delicious! Always remember when rock fishing, **never turn your back to the sea** — rogue waves can come in at any time and sweep you out.

Large rivers emptying into the sea are prime spots for kahawai, but they can be very dangerous areas depending on the weather, tides and the water flow, so be careful.

Redfin perch prefer slow-flowing and still water habitats.

FRESH WATER

Rivers, streams, lakes and ponds could all hold that monster fish you've been dreaming about. Don't think that you have to fish the biggest lake or a massive river either, as large fish can be found in small areas of water.

When a strong wind is blowing in exposed areas, then go looking for sheltered waterways such as deep creeks or drains, especially under willows.

Plan how to access the patch of water carefully and then drop the line in, slightly upstream. You have to decide if you are going to use a sinker, float or very light swivel attached to your line. A sinker will take the bait to the bottom. The float will keep the bait just below the surface. A **swivel** will provide just enough weight for the line, allowing it to sink slowly and the bait to drift downstream, gradually sinking as it goes and moving tantalisingly past the trout's nose, making it too attractive not to take.

A burley or bait sack can work well with perch, but has the tendency to bring around granddaddy eels which are a nuisance unless you are after them as well.

The very best way to understand exactly what a fish is eating is to gut one you have caught — this will reveal everything.

Check out the insect life in the water under rocks for bait. At the height of summer, cicadas hooked or tied to a hook

Tip:
Long-shank hooks are the easiest to use for freshwater fish such as trout and perch, both for baiting and getting the hooks out, because they provide much better grip. Hook sizes will vary according to the size of the fish's mouth, so once again anything from a 4/0 to a 10/0 might do the job.

and allowed to float down rapids on or near the surface can be very appealing to large trout. Grass grubs can be dug up or coaxed to the surface using a weak watery detergent mix poured down the surface holes, and works in minutes.

At all times of the year the humble worm on a short tied-on extension to the main line with a round sinker dropped under overhanging willows can be all you need.

If the smell of the bait doesn't do it for the fish, try exploring soft plastic or rubber imitations of crawlies, worms, grubs and beetles, as they can be incredibly lifelike in the water.

Tip:
A 'pigtail' or electric fence standard can be adjusted to form a brace holder for your rod very effectively.

OTHER GEAR YOU WILL NEED

A standard pocket knife will be versatile for cutting up bait, cutting nylon excess from knots and bleeding the fish with a cut under the gills. With care and if the blade is sharp enough, a pocket knife can do the job of **filleting** fish too. Get someone to show you how to fillet properly with a filleting knife if your prize fish is for the table — or simply take your time.

Always take spare hooks of varying sizes and a range of sinkers. As your interest in fishing grows, a **tackle** box can be added to

1. A general purpose bait cutting knife, excellent for a range of jobs. 2. Filleting knives with long, thin blades designed to cut the flesh into fillets. 3. A scaler for removing fish scales.

with all manner of handy equipment. There are tackle boxes for sale for under $40 containing a basic array of hooks, floats and lures which will set you up nicely. A **landing net** can easily be made out of an old tennis racket by cutting away the strings and sewing bird netting onto the frame in a sock-like shape.

If you're surfcasting a lot on a sandy beach, you might want to buy a rod holder to keep the reel out of the sand, as it gets tiring holding a surfcasting rod for a long time.

REGULATIONS

There are rules about the size and number of fish you are allowed to catch.

Kahawai: No limit on size or number
Herrings: No limit on size or number
Blue cod: 33 cm, apart from the Auckland region (30 cm)
Snapper: 27 cm
Trevally: 25 cm
Tarakihi: 25 cm
Gurnard: 25 cm

Check out www.fish.govt.nz for a full list of more fish species, specific regulations for certain areas, and numbers you are allowed to catch, or ask for the information at your local fishing store.

DID YOU KNOW?

- Blue cod is New Zealand's third most targeted species and can change its gender when conditions make it difficult to keep numbers up.
- Around 2500 tonnes, or 250,000 kilograms, of blue cod is commercially caught in New Zealand annually.
- Kahawai are only found in the Australasian region.
- The New Zealand coastline is 15,134 kilometres long. It is the ninth longest coastline in the world.
- The record size for a recreationally caught kahawai is ... 1.

GLOSSARY

Burley Bloody guts and fish offcuts thrown into the water to attract fish.

Cast The fishing term for throwing the line out.

Filleting The process of cutting fish flesh off the bones.

Landing net A net or mesh basket hoop used for scooping up fish near the surface.

Pikau A sack turned into a home-made pack.

Swivel A small device with two rings used to connect a fishing line to a leader line and hook.

Tackle Refers to everything from hooks to sinkers to nylon and swivels.

Trace A short piece of line attached to the main line with a hook tied on to the end.

A RECIPE TO TRY

BARBECUE PARCEL OF FISH

INGREDIENTS

1–2 fillets of fish per person
olive oil
1 lemon, sliced
1 tomato, sliced
black pepper and sea salt
fresh parsley and/or dill, chopped up
lemon juice
1 tsp butter per parcel

METHOD

1. Tear off a piece of tinfoil long enough to wrap 2 fillets in side by side.
2. Oil the tinfoil to stop the fillets sticking and to give flavour to the cooked fish.
3. On top of each fillet layer 2 lemon slices then 2 tomato slices.
4. Season with a sprinkle of black pepper and sea salt.
5. Sprinkle the chopped-up parsley and/ or dill on top of the lemon and tomato slices.
6. Squeeze the lemon juice over the top.
7. Add the butter to each parcel.
8. Seal the foil parcel by folding it like an envelope.
9. Place on the barbecue and cook both sides for 4 to 5 minutes.
10. Remove the parcel from the barbecue and leave to cool for a minute before opening. Be sure not to lean over the parcel as you open it because there may still be some steam inside.

SPINNING FOR TROUT AND PERCH

Of all the popular types of fishing from Northland to Southland, spinning is probably the most common next to bait fishing. By using a lure or spinner and following a few simple guidelines, you can successfully imitate a bait fish and entice a trout or perch from most of our rivers and lakes. And best of all, it requires only a few bits of equipment! A telltale bang on the line means you are both hooked – the fish on the spinner and you on the most exciting and wonderful recreational activity! For life!

BEFORE YOU FISH

Even though you can fish legally without a licence up to the age of 12, it's best to start by getting a junior version. You can go online to buy your licence (**www.fishandgame.org.nz**) and join the Fish & Game New Zealand national database. This helps to manage our valuable fishing resources and maintain them for the future.

WHERE TO FISH

Most of the major rivers in New Zealand are home to perch and trout. Smaller rivers and creeks are also worth checking out. Your local fishing store will be happy to help you, as every budding angler who experiences success will become a regular customer and pass on information about the sweet spots.

One of the hazards of spin fishing is snags, when your lure gets caught on rocks or logs. Even with experience, snags are an annoying fact of life. Using small, lighter lures in shallow water helps. The opposite is true for deeper water, where the lure needs to be heavier to get closer to the bottom to entice a fish. Look around the body of water before you cast. A disturbance on the surface of otherwise calm water could be a sign of a potential snag in the making.

The best places to fish tend to be where waterways meet — where creeks empty into larger rivers, or where rivers or small waterways empty into a lake. These are prime areas for either trout or perch as they snap up food carried by the flow of water.

Trout search out cooler water and slurp up insects, willow grubs and brown beetles falling from overhanging branches, so focus on the area beneath willows in summer. Trout will also often settle just at the section of water where the surface starts to ripple. They will dart forwards to take food carried by the current, or cruise backwards and forwards across the rapids. A spinner cast upstream and wound in to ensure

Tip:
When walking, always carry your rod with the tip angled towards the sky. This way you are less likely to damage or break your rod should you slip or fall on rocks or in mud.

HOW TO FISH

it curves with the water flow past such a turbulent section can be too hard to resist for a hungry trout.

Another great spot to investigate is where there are large boulders or tree trunks in the water — a perfect shelter from the current and a place to rest. The **eddy** created by such an obstacle also carries food directly to the resting fish! Be careful, though — if the fish are resting not far from the edge of the river, the last thing you want to do is wade out to cast into the deeper parts. You will just scare them away.

Trout will follow a **lure** right into the shallows. The lack of depth can work in your favour, as the fish will strike at the lure in desperation as it realises it is swimming into shallower water.

Trout tend to swim and feed alone, unlike perch which will feed in a group. They will occupy a stretch of water and boss everyone around like a schoolyard bully, chasing away or eating smaller fish. Be ready to act quickly with perch, as they can feed greedily for a time and then swiftly move off to other feeding areas. So get that line back into the water as fast as you can after each fish has been caught!

Trout and perch will often rest up during the main part of the day, making the most of the flow of the water carrying food towards

Tip:
Use a cheap pair of Polaroid sunglasses to help you spot fish in the water.

Rainbow Trout

Brown Trout

them. This helps them use the least amount of energy. Look out for likely spots as described on page 114.

Always look carefully over a stretch of water before moving closer, as three things can happen.

1. You can spot exactly where a fish is to plan your cast.
2. You can gain valuable information on what your fish is feeding on.
3. You can avoid scaring the fish into the rapids or down into the murky depths of a deep hole.

Know your prey: brown trout are cunning and know their habitat well. They will seek out every possible place where your line will snag, be it a boulder or fallen branches from a tree. Rainbow trout will seek the air, jumping spectacularly out of the water. They can throw the hook out of their mouths if you are not careful, so it is important that you keep the tension on the line, holding it tight, feeling the fish all the time. A loose line will only lead to disaster.

You do have to stalk trout, not just waltz up to the edge of the bank and expect them to hang around. Fish are sensitive to **vibrations**, so move carefully. When you are casting, think about landing the lure about half a metre upstream of the fish. This will help you to avoid snagging a lure, or splashing the spinner too close to the fish, scaring them off. The spinner will drift across in front of the fish as the current takes effect.

PRACTISING YOUR CAST

The key to casting your lure successfully is to focus on your landing spot. This takes practice!

Try it in your backyard first, but do not use a lure as that could be dangerous. Instead, attach a small round lead weight, as close to the weight of the lures you are mostly likely to use, and then get practising.

Set up targets, such as a hula hoop, and out of 20 casts from 10 metres, challenge yourself to beat your personal best.

Vary the distance to the target and keep a record of your scores — you will be surprised at how quickly the accuracy of your casting improves.

EQUIPMENT

A standard rod measures anywhere from 1.5 to 2.4 metres, although a rod from 1.7 metres to 2.4 metres will give you more choice at an affordable price. Rods are usually made up of two pieces but can be bought as three or four pieces for easy storage.

Comfortable clothing and a spare set of warm clothes is essential, especially if you're fishing early in the morning or in the late afternoon and into the evening, as the temperature can drop quickly. The clothes you wear should blend in with your surroundings. Ideally you should wear subdued colours so you are not highly visible. Fish, particularly trout, are very territorial. They will stay in a section of river for as long they can until their food supply runs out. They get to know their backyard extremely well, and will soon spot sudden or unusual movements, or brightly dressed anglers, and will beat a hasty retreat to deeper water or nearby rapids.

Take a camera with you to record any fish you choose to release. More and more anglers are choosing to catch and release fish and will only take one fish home for supper. To catch and release without hurting the fish, you need to take the barb off the hook. This can be done by using a pair of long-nosed pliers to squeeze or cut the barb off or squash it down. Once you have done this it is far easier to simply slip the hook out of a fish's mouth.

Before touching the fish you must also wet your hands, otherwise your warm, dry skin can burn their skin and result in the fish dying. Some anglers carry a nylon sock or stocking which they slip over their hand, soak in the water, and then carefully handle the fish before releasing.

Allow the fish to adjust to the water when you catch and release — don't just heave them back in with a big old slap. Keep them upright and facing upstream, allowing the current to flow back through their gills, and, as they get stronger and more active, release them.

triple hook

beads

spinner

LURES

Always check the nylon close to the lure for smoothness, and ensure the knot is secure. There is nothing worse than hooking the local monster of a fish only to have your line snap! If you have any doubts about the strength or condition of the nylon, which can weaken with overuse, or wear away after contact with stones and logs, you should cut off the lure and move down the nylon a few centimetres or so. Practise your fishing knots and re-attach the spinner.

Try tying a red or yellow bead near the spinner as an added attraction, especially if you are not getting any bites. Trout and perch love these colours, and perch have been known to go for yellow gorse flowers with a hook threaded through. This works well at the height of summer with light lures lazily cast under willows.

The good old Black and Gold Toby spinner works for perch time and again.

Trout have a huge range of spinners, but the Gold Toby or anything with gold is effective.

Home-made lures require a triple hook, swivel, two ring clips and something you want to use as the body of the spinner — anything shiny that you can safely drill a hole at either end will work well.

Remember that trout and perch will follow a spinner right up to the water's edge a lot of the time, and in desperation will strike your spinner just before the water gets too shallow. You don't need to seek out the deepest water to catch your fish.

Lures that have spinning attachments can be very helpful in low-visibility water, as the fish can sense the vibrations from the spin. These lures can be wound in more slowly. Their action in the water also keeps them up off the bottom, and this allows the fish more time to find and strike the lure. Brightly coloured and shinier lures and spinners are also generally effective in low-visibility water as they are more easily spotted by hungry trout. In cleaner and clearer waters, lures that are more naturally coloured can

Tip:
Keep your lure hooks sharp by running a small file over the points. Rocks and boulders can make their edges blunt.

be more effective as they imitate the trout's prey more realistically.

RIVERS ARE KILLERS

Rivers are a major source of drowning in New Zealand every year. When crossing rivers there are a number of things you need to think about:

1. How deep is it?
2. How fast is the flow?
3. What angle must you take to get to the other side?
4. Do you need to get into the water in the first place?

Read back over the 'River crossing strategies' section on pages 66–67.

DID YOU KNOW?

- A trout caught in 2012 from the Ohau sea canal out of Twizel weighed in at a whopping 17.9 kilograms.
- Brown trout were introduced to New Zealand in 1860 and rainbow trout in 1883.
- Perch were brought to New Zealand in 1860.
- Perch love the colour red and can reach up to 2.2 kilograms.

GLOSSARY

Eddy A patch of water behind boulders or logs where the water current swirls and flows more slowly.

Lure Another name for a spinner.

Polaroid Treated glass which reduces the glare on the surface of the water.

Vibrations The movements detected by fish as the angler treads on stones and gravel.

A RECIPE TO TRY

BAKED WHOLE TROUT

INGREDIENTS

1 large trout
2 tbsp melted butter
4 lemon slices
2 tbsp lemon pepper seasoning
olive oil (cold pressed) for drizzling

METHOD

1. Preheat oven to 180°C.

2. Line a large baking dish with tinfoil.

3. Split open your fish, brush the melted butter inside, then add 2 slices of lemon and sprinkle over the lemon pepper seasoning.

4. Close your fish and place the remaining lemon slices on top.

5. Completely cover the fish in tinfoil and bake for about 15 minutes, checking it regularly until the flesh flakes easily.

6. Remove from the oven, uncover the fish and drizzle with olive oil.

EELING OUR WATERWAYS

There are two types of eel in New Zealand: shortfin and longfin. They are great fun to hunt and catch, but their population, especially the longfin eel, is also in gradual decline. If you are hunting to eat, do check how many eels you are permitted to catch and take in your region. Eels are protected by our Quota Management System, which ensures our fish stocks are sustained for the future. Both species of eel in New Zealand take a long time to grow and can live for as long as 60 years, so it is important that we hunt them wisely. Do consider catch and release if you do not need to hunt them for food.

WHERE TO GO EELING

You can find eels in just about every waterway across New Zealand, from shallow farm drains, to creeks and streams. You can also find them in the shallows of rivers, where the water is only 10 centimetres deep, as well as in river holes up to 5 metres deep and in the darker depths of lakes and farm dams. Hunt under bridges or overhanging willows where the water is cooler and where eels live in holes along the banks.

HOW TO CATCH EELS

There are a number of ways to catch eels without killing them.

SPEAR OR GAFF

Spearing or using a **gaff** is usually done by spotlight at night, but can be done in daylight by stalking weeds along river banks or by using bait as a lure.

To create your own burley, mix stale bread with any leftovers you have to hand. A couple of old duck eggs or a rabbit or possum carcass will have eels coming from kilometres downstream. Sheep guts from a local farmer are ideal dangled in a sack with small holes cut in it to let the blood and smell out.

Tie the sack to a bridge or to a stake in the ground upstream from your fishing spot. You can spear or gaff them as they swim by. Using fishing lines in the water can also work very well.

There is no catch and release with this method, so a decision has to be made: Are you going to kill and eat the eels?

You can attach a spear head to an old broom handle to make an eel spear.

HAND NET

Hand nets can work especially well with smaller eels. Stand near the water's edge and place your net downstream, in the path of the most likely escape route, then overturn a boulder or log. Always do this slowly, as the natural water flow will flush away disturbed or dirty water and any fish underneath will often hang around just that little bit longer, giving you enough time to make any adjustments with the net to scoop them up.

To make a basic hand net, use a standard broom handle with a number 8 wire loop at one end. You can even use an old tennis racket frame, with anything from old stockings or bird netting from the garden centre for the net. Wrap the net around the frame and use simple in-and-out stitching to hold it in place.

The beauty of the hand-net method is that the eel can be scooped up and safely landed on the river bank. You can take photographs and then return the eel unharmed to its home.

Tip:
Warning! Eels bite! Use a sack to cover your hands, then pick them up carefully using both hands. The cloth will stop the slimy creature from squeezing and slithering through your fingers.

FISHING ROD OR HAND LINE

Using a fishing rod or hand line to catch an eel can be hard: once you land an eel it will twist and writhe around and tangle your line — so be prepared.

Eels caught on rods with a light nylon line can be a handful, especially if the eel is large. It will bang its head from side to side and twist around. Even very small eels can fight really hard and cause major line tangles.

Hand lines are much easier to manage, particularly if you use string or cord, as they do not tangle so much. You can set your hand line overnight (see page 126), using a good-sized piece of juicy meat with gristle to attract the eels.

To reduce any harm to the eel and enable a quick release after you have taken a photograph, squash or cut off the barbs on the hooks you use.

Basic rigs include string hand lines with a heavy sinker at the very end of the line and a hook attached about 30 centimetres

Tip:
To avoid smaller eels or fish nibbling bait, wrap a short piece of cotton around and around the bait to protect it.

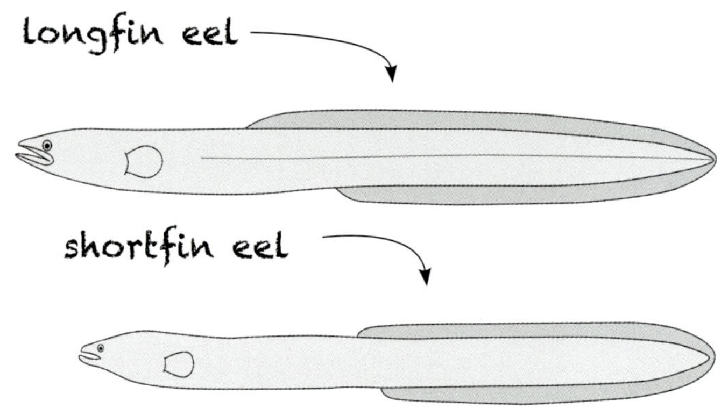

One way to tell the difference between the longfin and shortfin is by looking at their fins. The length of a longfin's dorsal fin (the top fin) extends further toward the head than the shortfin's dorsal.

above the sinker. It pays to have the hook attached on a short trace out from the main line. This allows the eel to swallow the hook more easily, as it is attached away from the main line.

Early Maori used to strip flax into fine lengths and tie it around and around bait, making a furry ball. An eel has many layers of teeth that face back towards their throat, and so they find it very hard to get their teeth out of something once they have bitten into it. As soon as the bait was taken, their teeth would be caught in the flax fibres and they were quickly captured and pulled up onto the bank.

A similar method can be used with nylon pantyhose wrapped around bait. Using this approach means you do not have the job of removing a hook from the eel!

In New Zealand we are facing a drastic fall in the number of longfin eels, especially the older and larger eels which are more likely to breed. Consider yourself a true conservationist — take a photo and return the eel to the water.

Tip:
To remove the hook quickly, have a sack or old length of material at the ready. Use it to wrap the eel and provide you with a better grip on their slippery skin.

SET LINE

Using a hand line and setting it overnight can be highly effective. Eels will travel long distances during the night, and the smell from your bait may take time to entice an eel to the hook. Make sure you anchor the line firmly, as a big eel could easily spin and twist it from the water's edge.

This method, while effective, means that you will probably have to kill your catch. The eel will digest the hook and bait. Removing the hook without seriously harming the eel is unlikely, but you could cut the line and release the eel.

HINAKI OR EEL TRAP

Early Maori used to make hinaki, or eel traps, out of flax. You can make one out of chicken netting and number 8 wire. If you can find a good spot and set your trap overnight, the hinaki will be alive with squirming eel tails as you pull it out of the water.

It is important to set your trap with the opening facing downstream, as this is the direction from where the eels will seek out your bait and swim. Make sure the bait is right at the top end of your trap and away from the sides! The eels will happily feed away all night on what they can reach. Always anchor your trap with a length of rope, as rising water overnight can sweep it away.

Tip:
Eels will usually release the bait once they are on the bank.

SPOTLIGHTING

Spotlighting for eels at night is great fun and is usually done in more shallow water. Drains and creeks are ideal, as the whole area from bank to bank can be covered with the light from one torch.

Headlamps are an excellent idea, as your hands will be free to bait hooks and line up your spear. Having your hands free also means you will be more balanced and less likely to fall into the water!

Tip:
Use bait that will stay on the hook, as little eels are great at nibbling away your bait before a bigger eel can get to it.

BAIT

Eels will eat pretty much anything! Any gristly offcut from beef, venison or hare is perfect. Hare meat is darker than rabbit and seems to give off a stronger scent in the water. Cheese can also work well, but it needs to be tied on.

SAFETY

Always go eeling with a friend or family member, never by yourself. Always tell someone exactly where you are fishing and when you will be home.

PREPARING AND EATING EELS

One of the best ways to prepare eels is to smoke them. To do this you gut the eel, peel back its skin and rub brown sugar on the flesh. You then smoke the eel by hanging it on a hook in an open-fire chimney.

Eels can also be cut crossways into steaks, rubbed with olive oil and pepper, and fried on the barbecue. As eel is very rich, you won't need much to get your fill.

Mature eel leave their freshwater homes and head to the sea to breed. Early Maori dug long trenches in the sand at the mouth of an estuary, at the point where eels would pass to reach the ocean. Rather than swim out to sea, the trenches led the eel to shallow ponds where they were speared, gutted and laid out on racks to dry. Dried eel ensured a sustained food supply over long winter months.

DID YOU KNOW?

- Longfin eels can live to more than 60 years old.
- The largest recorded eel was over 40 kilograms.
- Eels are great upstream swimmers and can climb dam walls or banks of up to 6 metres.
- Mature eels migrate down our creeks and rivers and out to sea. They travel hundreds of kilometres to an area of ocean near Tonga to breed.
- Eel blood is toxic to humans.
- Eels have poor eyesight and are generally nocturnal.
- In parts of French Polynesia, eels are considered sacred.
- There are about 800 species of eel all around the world.

GLOSSARY

Gaff A curved, hook-like tool with a sharp point designed to hook and pierce the fish as it is pulled out of the water.

Quota A share of the total, the amount you are allowed to take.

THE WONDERS OF WHITEBAITING

Whitebait is a tender, luxurious treat. People will go to enormous efforts to catch whitebait, or 'white gold' or 'New Zealand's caviar' as it is also known. At the start of whitebait season there is always excitement and anticipation. You will see young and not-so-young standing shoulder to shoulder on river banks searching for this tiny, silvery, delicately thin fish.

WHAT IS WHITEBAIT?

Whitebait is the juvenile or immature fry of our freshwater fish. They are usually between 25 to 50 millimetres long, and can be found in our creeks, rivers and lakes. When caught in the bottom of a net they look like long silvery slithers.

There are five main species that can make up a whitebait catch. The most common of all is the inanga. The second species is the koaro. The banded kokopu, shortjaw kokopu and giant kokopu complete the famous five. We often refer to all of these fish as cockabullies, and can catch them in hand nets and buckets from our local waterways.

The fertilised eggs of these fish hatch at high tide. The larvae sweep with the falling tide down creeks and rivers into the sea, where the hatchlings spend the winter. As juveniles, or whitebait, they begin their migratory journey back from the sea into our rivers. Spring is the time to catch them.

In the early days, before refrigeration, the whitebait catch was rushed off to canneries. Lots of makeshift airstrips were hacked out of the bush on the South Island's West Coast so that planes could transport the precious cargo to the market as quickly as possible.

On the mighty Waikato River in the late 1850s, Maori had to pay one penny per pound of hao inanga, or whitebait, as a form of moni ika, or whitebait tax. This money did not go to the government, but was delivered to Kingitanga, the Maori King movement, to ensure the institution was maintained.

Shortjaw kokopu.

WHEN TO WHITEBAIT

Whitebait can be hard to find. You never know what date or time they will enter rivers. The whitebait season usually opens on 15 August, but be sure to check your region's official date each year (see 'Rules and regulations' on page 137).

The best time to set a net is when there has been a 'spring tide'. Spring tides have nothing to do with the spring season: these tides are a result of the moon, sun and

Earth being aligned, or in line, with each other. This alignment creates a stronger than normal gravitational pull on the oceans, which results in very high and very low tides.

Just as the full moon has a magnetic pull on whitebait to venture upriver, so does the excitement of the season draw whitebaiters, like a gold rush, to the coast, with utes, car trailers and caravans stacked high with nets.

Older whitebaiters say that the first couple of 'freshes', or small floods, can entice the whitebait up and into our rivers. The dirtier water at the river mouth also helps the whitebaiter, as the juvenile fish remain unaware of the nets until they have been scooped up.

Seabirds are another of Nature's whitebait indicators: gulls and smaller terns will hover just above the surf, diving in regularly as they spot a juicy morsel.

This is a perfect time to double up on your fishing opportunities: kahawai, sea-run trout and mullet will also be hunting the whitebait.

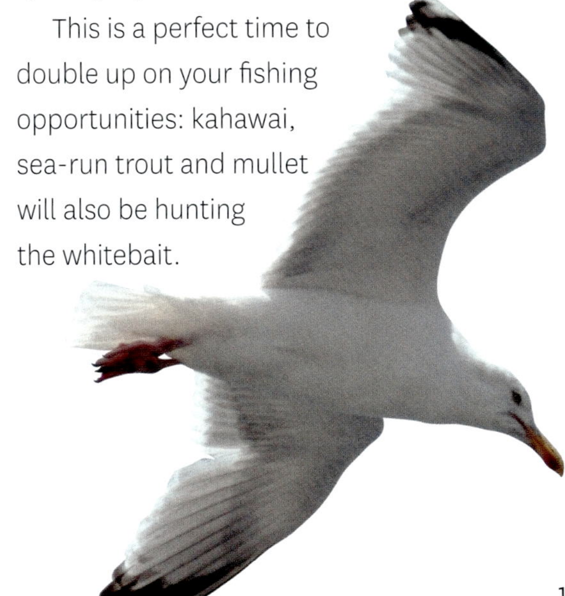

HOW TO WHITEBAIT

Depending on where you are fishing and the visibility of the water, it is better to wear subdued or camouflage clothing. Whitebait have good eyesight, and, due to the fact that they are being chased all day by marauding fish and birds, the slightest of movements can send them scattering, usually to deeper water which is much harder to fish.

There are two main methods of fishing for whitebait, depending on the area you are fishing. The size, flow and power of the water will dictate which method you use.

SCOOPING

The scooping method requires strength, effort and lots of attention to safety. It involves scooping each wave as it ripples in at the mouth of the river as the incoming tide rolls in. **Never do this type of fishing on your own** as it can be extremely dangerous. Rogue waves at a river mouth can meet and combine with a fresh (small flood) coming down the river, and this can dramatically change the depth of the shingle underfoot, easily throwing you off your balance.

The Rakaia scoop is named after the mighty Rakaia River on the West Coast of the South Island, and has been developed over the years as technology and materials have advanced. It has been designed to deal with the fast-flowing pebbly river bottom, much the same as the scoop designs for the Lake Ferry region in the Wairarapa.

Tip:
Tie a lead weight to the lower tube using wheel rim weights from a service station. You can also place lead weights inside the lower tube before joining it up.

A short pole is attached to a rigid scoop made out of light metal reinforcing rods and padded with hosing or **alkathene tubing**. The mesh, which is like fly-screen material only much stronger, is robust enough to withstand the wear and tear caused by thousands of scoops over rough stones.

Other types of nets include triangular frames simply held at the top of the net mouth and swung into the waves as the whitebait come through. This means you will bend more to complete each sweep. Use your powerful leg muscles to support you and protect your back. If the waves gather momentum, do take care! You don't want to scoop too deeply into each wave. This will definitely give you a good workout!

Another method of scooping is to drag a lightweight net through the waves just back from the mouth of the river. These nets are usually used on sandy bottoms and in shallower water. A sock net, which is attached to 40 or 50 millimetre PVC tubing which you join at the corners with simple elbows, is cheap to buy from a sports store.

EQUIPMENT

Most whitebaiters will wear waders. **Neoprene** waders are considerably safer than others, even if others are more flexible, as the angler can simply allow their legs to float up if they find themselves out of their depth. **Remember to always wear a life-jacket and always go with others: it's more fun and a whole lot safer.**

SET NET

With a set net you will usually be further upriver, carefully arranging what are called 'gobys', or small fences, with the set net. The effort needed here is largely in the setting up of the equipment, but once in place you can sit back and relax, or even bait up your rods and get lines in the water. The river bed ideally suited to set nets can vary from a shallow, consistent sandy bottom to a

Tip:
Add a lead sinker at the very end of the net to keep it from flowing back on itself.

deeper, unsteady pebble base.

Longer pole nets can be used in deeper water. A swimming pool scoop-pole can be telescoped down and easily packed on the roof-rack or in the trailer. In faster-flowing water a more robust pole made out of a length of manuka or aluminium is required. The net material has a knot tied towards the end to form a trap so the whitebait can't escape.

On some stretches of West Coast rivers and creeks, large box nets are placed out into the deep water.

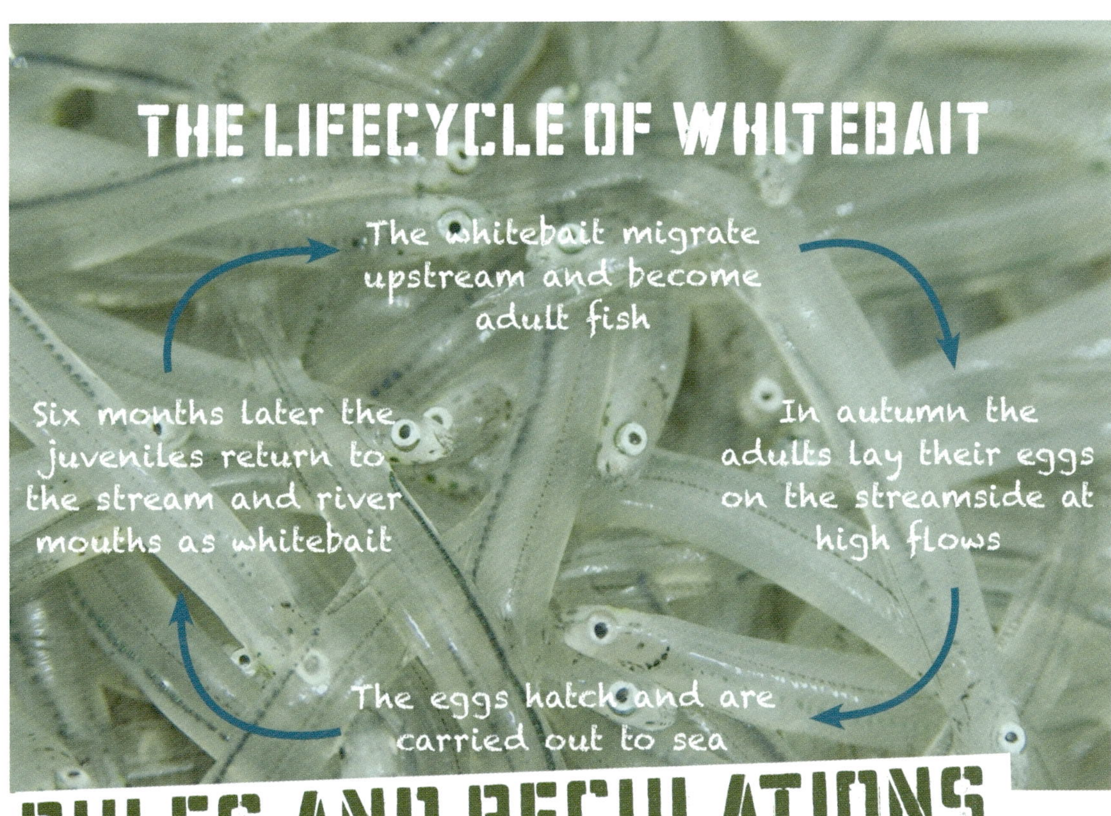

RULES AND REGULATIONS

Season dates are usually 15 August to 30 November, from 5 a.m. to 8 p.m. daily or 6 a.m. to 9 p.m. when daylight saving begins. The West Coast has a different season, running from 1 September to 14 November. Nets should not be higher than 1 metre at the opening. They must be flat-bottomed and must be no longer than 3.5 metres. On any water channel you are not allowed to fence off more than one-third of the waterway's width, even when you are with another person.

Make sure you check out other requirements in the helpful booklet *The Whitebaiter's Guide to Whitebait* which you can get from DOC or your local fishing store.

Tip:
Baby flounder, herrings and even shrimp will sometimes turn up in your net. A small fish called smelt may wind up in your catch, too. These fish give off a smell of cucumber. Often whitebaiters will pick smelt out of the net and throw them back, but you may want to hang onto them if you have enough, as, dipped in flour and fried in butter, smelt are excellent for supper.

DID YOU KNOW?

- The life cycle of whitebait is influenced by the spring tides. They begin their long migratory journey from the sea to the rivers when these tides take place.
- When whitebait is in short supply it can cost up to $180 per kilogram!
- Giant kokopu and shortjaw kokopu are monitored carefully by DOC. The species are under threat due to overfishing and destruction of their native habitat.
- Whitebait exports are worth an annual $1.1 billion to New Zealand.
- Be careful: you may catch juvenile eels that look like whitebait but they are very light brown and wriggle differently in the bucket. They are very precious, so let them go straight away.
- Didymo, that awful sludge that attaches to rocks in our rivers and is often called 'rock snot', can easily be transported from river to river if you don't wash all your gear carefully. Help look after our rivers.

GLOSSARY

Alkathene tubing The black irrigation hose used on farms and in garden watering systems.

Neoprene Synthetic rubber material used in waders and wetsuits.

A RECIPE TO TRY

WHITEBAIT FRITTERS

INGREDIENTS

1 cup whitebait

1 egg

1 heaped tbsp flour

salt and pepper to taste (a grind of each is good)

1 tbsp butter

1 tbsp olive oil

white bread to serve

lemon wedges to serve

METHOD

1. Place the whitebait in a sieve and wash under a cold tap. Gently shake dry.

2. In a small bowl, whisk the egg until it is light and fluffy.

3. Add the flour and salt and pepper to the egg. Whisk them together until you have a smooth batter.

4. Add the washed and dried whitebait to the batter. Fold through very gently.

5. Heat a frying pan on medium heat. Add the butter and olive oil. The olive oil will stop the butter from burning, which will give your fritter a bitter taste.

6. Add 2 tablespoons of the mixture for each fritter.

7. Cook for 2 to 3 minutes until the fritter is golden on the bottom.

8. Carefully turn each fritter over and cook for another 2 minutes.

9. Be careful not to overcook or it will be tough. (They are cooked when your finger doesn't leave a dent in the middle of the fritter when pressed down gently.)

10. Serve on a slice of soft white bread with a wedge of lemon to squeeze over the top, and salt and pepper to season if you want.

ACKNOWLEDGEMENTS

My sincere thanks go to Alex Hedley at Random House, for his superb enthusiasm for the concept of a kid's book on hunting and fishing and his untiring support and attention to detail.

To my wonderful wife, Suzie, a legend for her opening morning hampers bursting with every imaginable goodie; for her proof-reading skills and boundless ideas, not to mention endless cups of coffee and recipe experiments!

To James and Tom, our two fantastic sons who share the same passion for the outdoors and respect for our wildlife; thanks for your brilliant company, input, ideas and help with the photo-shoots.

To Don Humphrey, my stalwart hunting companion of many years, from Stewart Island to the Kaimanawas, thanks for the yarns, invaluable input and ideas, and for giving the text the once-over.

To Chris Day, who shares my enthusiasm for getting kids out into the great outdoors, and was also prepared to read through this book offering ideas or advice, many thanks.

To Mike Heydon for capturing the very essence of our great outdoors with his incredible photos — we see it the same!

To Adrienne McLachlan and Paul Gatland of the New Zealand Police, thank you for your careful checking of the gun safety aspects.

To Tony Roseingrave of Sportsworld King & Henry Masterton, thanks for allowing us to spend a day in your shop photographing hunting and fishing equipment.

To Ian Buick of the Masterton Smallbore Association, who was a great source of information and a kindred spirit regarding a safe introduction to hunting. Much appreciated, Ian.

To my parents, Brian and Lily, for always encouraging me to pursue my love of the outdoors and exploring new areas to hunt or fish.

Finally to Uncle Jim, who gave me my first Labrador 'Bosun' and took me out on those afternoon rabbit hunts which set me on my journey to enjoy all there is about safe and ethical hunting in our incredible backyard. Thanks 'Unc'!

IMAGE CREDITS

123RF: 54 (bottom), 82 (bottom), 122, 134 (bottom).

Alexander Turnbull Library: 26 (top, ref: PAColl-8210. Photograph of rabbit pelts in store awaiting sale, creator unknown), 26 (bottom, ref: PA11-162-001. Boy and Aubrey Whitcombe, after rabbit hunting, Catlins River, Otago. Edgar Richard Williams, 1891–1983), 33 (top, ref: PAColl-8983-01. Duck shooting from a maimai on Lake Ellesmere, Canterbury. New Zealand Free Lance), 39 (top, ref: WA-25274-G. Duck shooting, featuring dead ducks strung up on rack, location unknown. Whites Aviation Ltd), 39 (bottom, ref: 1/2-010367-G. Shooting party at Shag Cove, Pelorus Sound. Frederick James Halse, d. 1936), 57 (ref: PAColl-8983-05. Caption: Two possum trappers with a day's catch from the Lake Waikaremoana district. New Zealand Free Lance), 73 (ref: PA1-o-738-13. Arthur Gregg on hillside with gun and dead deer. Frederick William Furkert, 1876–1949), 75 (bottom left, ref: PAColl-0001-2-1-006. Cyril Rutland going pighunting, Mokau River. Robert E Wells, 1905–2006), 85 (bottom, ref: 1/4-057820-G. Two wild pigs and rifle lying on rock. Robert E Wells, 1905–2006), 87 (left, ref: 1/2-113515-F. Man with a rifle and a wild pig, Manukau Heads. A G McLaren), 87 (right, ref: 1/2-100198-G. Hunter with deer. New Zealand Free Lance), 93 (bottom, ref: 114/389/15-G. Archery contest. Negatives of the Evening Post newspaper), 97 (bottom, ref: 1/2-211597-F. People with archery arrows. K E Niven and Co), 99 (top, ref: WA-10172-G. Summer Child Studies series, three unidentified boys, fishing. Whites Aviation Ltd), 106 (right, ref: 1/2-228411-F. Children fishing off wharf. K E Niven and Co), 109 (bottom middle, ref: 1/1-004934-G. Fishing, Northland. Northwood brothers), 109 (bottom right, ref: 114/117/12-G. Men with 234-pound bass fish caught in Cook Strait, Wellington. Negatives of the Evening Post newspaper), 110 (ref: PAColl-0477-16. Maori children by a catch of trout. James Ingram McDonald, 1865–1935), 118 (left, ref: WA-04366-G. Trout fishing, Grace's Reach, Tongariro River. Whites Aviation Ltd), 127 (top left, ref: PA1-q-002-083. Eel-basket (hinaki) constructed of tokororaro vine, at the Hokio Stream, mua-upoko craftsmanship, 29 November 1925. George Leslie Adkin, 1888–1964), 127 (top right, ref: 1/1-007414-G. Traditional Maori wicker baskets for trapping eels and other fish. Samuel Heath Head, d. 1948), 128 (right, ref: A-076-016. Catching the legendary eel at Tangahoe, 1938?. Thomas William Downes, 1868–1938), 129 (top, ref: PA1-q-257-73-1. Photograph of a wicker fishing trap or pot (hinaki). James Ingram McDonald, 1865–1935), 129 (middle, ref: 1/2-026559-G. Eel catchers. Frederick Nelson Jones, 1881–1962), 129 (bottom, ref: WA-26446-F. Unidentified boy dangling an eel on some fishing line, Maraetai, Auckland. Whites Aviation Ltd), 131 (top, ref: WA-25215-G. Whitebaiting, featuring unidentified Maori boy with whitebait net on banks of unidentified river, Bay of Plenty Region. Whites Aviation Ltd), 136 (top, ref: PAColl-8983-03. R. Biddington placing whitebait nets in the Taramakau River, West Coast region. New Zealand Free Lance), 136 (middle, ref: PAColl-6388-95. Whitebaiting, Grey River. New Zealand Free Lance), 138 (ref: APG-1581-1/2-G. Henry Gurr and his son whitebaiting on the Taieri River. Albert Percy Godber, 1875–1949).

Alex Hedley: 50 (top right), 53, 98.

Chris Day: 113 (top).

Emma Hodder: 19 (left), 30 (top left), 101 (bottom left), 126.

iStock: 92 (ref: 1664326).

Keith Maclean: 85 (middle).

Mike Heydon: 1–15, 18, 20 (left), 21 (top and bottom left), 22 (top), 27 (bottom), 30 (top right), 31, 35, 36 (top), 47 (left), 50 (bottom), 55 (left), 58, 62–63, 64 (top), 66 (right), 74 (right), 84 (right), 85 (top), 89, 96, 100, 102, 103 (bottom), 108 (bottom), 114 (right), 116 (left), 119 (bottom), 120, 124 (bottom), 127 (bottom right).

Nelson Provincial Museum: 16 (Kingsford Collection, ref: 1/4 369B).

Paul Adamson: 17, 22 (bottom), 24, 27 (middle left), 37 (top), 38, 41, 55 (right), 74 (left), 83 (left), 92 (right), 94 (top), 104 (top right), 111, 114 (left), 125, 127 (bottom left).

Photos.com: 19, 21 (bottom right), 27 (top and middle right), 28–29, 32 (top), 33 (bottom), 34, 36 (bottom), 37 (bottom), 40, 42, 44, 45 (top), 46, 49, 52 (top), 54 (top), 59–61, 64 (bottom left and bottom right), 66 (left), 67–70, 72, 75 (top and bottom right), 76–77, 79, 80 (top), 81, 82 (middle), 90–91, 93 (top), 94 (bottom), 95, 97 (top left and right), 101 (top and bottom right), 104 (left and bottom right), 105, 106 (left), 107, 108 (top), 109 (top and bottom left), 113 (bottom), 115, 116 (right), 117, 118 (right), 119 (top), 121, 132 (top and bottom), 133, 135, 137.

Photo New Zealand: 103 (top:, ref: 215161, Terry Hann), 123 (ref: 321904, Rob Tucker), 124 (top right, ref: 331504, Rob Tucker), 136 (bottom, ref: 327926, Rob Tucker).

Piers Fuller: 51.

Rob Suisted: 20 (right, ref: 31569LR00. Dropping pile of European Rabbit), 43 (top, ref: 27511BI00. Starling bird in breeding plumage), 43 (bottom, ref: 41547BI00. Common blackbird digging for insects in winter garden. Widespread introduced species to New Zealand), 45 (bottom, ref: 17221FG10. Predator/stoat trapping tunnels, with a freeze-dried rat as bait and the cover removed for viewing, at Te Urewera National Park), 48 (ref: 2950LO01. Possum standing upright, Gollans Valley, Wellington), 50 (top left, ref: 22826LO03. Possum bite marks on Putaputaweta tree bark, Lake Waikaremoana), 52 (bottom, ref: 2951LO01. Timms possum trap with dead possum in it, Gollans Valley, Wellington), 78 (ref: 7480LF07. Wild Red deer 'spiker' in thick bush), 80 (bottom, ref: 39044HG00. Hunter roaring or bugling for rutting deer on tussock tops above Lake Alice, Edith River, Fiordland National Park), 82 (top, ref: 26862HT00. Dead young whitetail deer buck with five-point antlers and hunting rifle, Stewart Island), 83 (right, ref: 37733HP00. Pig hunting dog focussed on the hunt, Masterton), 84 (left, ref: 39337LG00. Wild goat herd amongst native coastal vegetation), 112 (ref: 45750RJ00. Trout fishing in Bowscale Tarn, Sedgemere, Marlborough), 124 (top left, ref: 5668FF01. Longfin eel on river bottom, Mt Bruce, Masterton), 128 (left, ref: 18124FF05. Longfin eels swimming out of underwater logs), 130 (ref: 35243RF00. Whitebait fishing at Waikanae River mouth, Kapiti Coast), 131 (bottom, ref: 35223FF00. Juvenile or larval form of the inanga or adult whitebait fish), 132 (middle, ref: 7286FF02. Native shortjawed Kokopu, Taranaki), 134 (top, ref: 27947FF06. Whitebait fisherman checking net, Waikanae), 139 (ref: 31581FF00. Whitebait fritter).

Wairarapa Archives: 71 (ref: 10-200-002).

INDEX

Q

R

S

T

WINCHESTER
SUPER-X
Ranger
25 PLASTIC SHOT SHELLS
Remington
Gun Club
Target Loads
ROYAL
STEEL
RIO
25 PLASTIC SHOTGUN SHELLS
hunter
Hunting
PMC
Steel Shot
Remington
B&P
Magnum Steel
CLUB 28
25 TRAP CARTRIDGES
TARGET LOAD
CLUB
32
UNO
GB
SUPER EXPRESS
36
CAZA
WINCHESTER
ELEY
MAXIMUM
WINCHESTER
SUPER-X
BUSHMAN
FIOCCHI